The Overthinker's Guide to Making Decisions

BOOKS BY JOSEPH NGUYEN:

Don't Believe Everything You Think: Why Your Thinking Is the Beginning & End of Suffering (Expanded Edition)

Beyond Thoughts: An Exploration of Who We Are Beyond Our Minds

The Art of Creating: How to Create Art That Transforms Yourself and the World

You may find my books, courses, and newsletter on my website: josephnguyen.org

The Overthinker's Guide to Making Decisions

How to Make Decisions Without Losing Your Mind

Joseph Nguyen

AUTHORS EQUITY

/≣

Authors Equity
1123 Broadway, Suite 1008
New York, New York 10010

Edited by Cecily van Buren-Freedman
Cover design by Jared Oriel
Book design by Studiolo Secondari

Library of Congress Control Number: 2025941029
Print ISBN 9798893310665
Ebook ISBN 9798893310825

Printed in the United States of America
First Printing

www.authorsequity.com

Most Authors Equity books are available at a discount when purchased in quantity for sales promotions or corporate use. Special editions, which include personalized covers, excerpts, and corporate imprints, can be created when purchased in large quantities. For more information, please email info@authorsequity.com.

Contents

I.
A New Way to Decide

Rethinking Everything We Know
About Making Decisions

"Choices are the hinges of destiny."
—EDWIN MARKHAM

"We need to accept that we won't always make the right decisions, that we'll screw up royally sometimes—understanding that failure is not the opposite of success, it's part of success."

—ARIANNA HUFFINGTON

Chapter 1

The Silent Weight of Choice

"When something bad happens you have three choices. You can either let it define you, let it destroy you, or you can let it strengthen you."

—DR. SEUSS

One of the greatest powers we possess is choice, the ability to consciously choose one path over another. With this, we hold the power to reshape the course of our lives in an instant—something few, if any, other life-forms appear to do in the same way.

But with this great power comes great suffering.

Far too easily, we find ourselves trapped in indecision, a paralysis caused not by limitation, but by infinite possibility. The culprit is not too little choice, but too much. And so, we end up suffering, not because we lack options, but because we drown in them.

Heavy is the head that wears the crown of choice.

The pressure to make the *right* decision can feel overwhelming, not because the choice is impossibly complex, but because the stakes of choosing wrong feel so high. In these moments, what we feel is determined not by the size of the decision, but by the gravity of our emotions. When the mind spirals, even the smallest choice can feel like a heavy burden, as if so much depends on it.

What begins as a simple decision doesn't stay that way for long. As we contemplate different outcomes, our mind fixates on the negative. One wrong decision, we realize, and everything could fall apart—the job we worked so hard for, the love we were just beginning to trust, the fragile peace we fought to find, the chance we thought might change everything.

But it's not just bad outcomes we fear; it's the perception of others. The silence in the room. The shift in someone's tone. The look in their eyes when they no longer see us the same.

What if we lose their respect? What if we lose their love? What if the people we care about most no longer believe in us?

We can see it unfolding in our mind's eye as clear as day: choose "wrong," and suddenly the job disappears, the relationship crumbles, our reputation shatters, and the voice in our head taunts: *See? You never deserved this.*

That's the risk that feels the highest—not the practical consequence, but the way a bad decision seems to serve as evidence of our deepest fears about ourselves. A "wrong" decision doesn't just feel like a mistake; it feels like confirmation. Confirmation that we're not capable enough. Not wise enough. Not enough.

Before we know it, the worry has spiraled out of control, and what may have started as a small decision has now become an existential crisis.

And so, we find ourselves seeking advice, not necessarily for clarity, but for reassurance. Maybe if enough people tell us what to do, the weight of choosing will disappear. We silently hope—perhaps without even realizing it—that someone else will decide for us. Because if the choice ends up being a mistake, it won't be our fault, it will be theirs. After all, it's far easier to live resenting someone else's decision than it is to bear the consequences of our own.

But the more we rely on these opinions, the heavier the decision becomes. Now, in addition to the need to make the "right" choice, we must contend with the pressure to please.

This is how the burden grows. You weigh your desires against the expectations of others, feeling the quiet guilt of all they've given you. How could you possibly choose a path they don't agree with? How could you risk disappointing the very people who have supported you? It's easy to convince yourself that prioritizing what feels right for you is selfish.

And yet, if making everyone else happy were the key to your own happiness, wouldn't it have worked by now?

The truth is that the more voices we invite in, the quieter our internal voice becomes.

Each opinion, no matter how well intended, pulls us further from the still, inner knowing we already sense.

Everyone offers what they think is best, yet none of them can tell you what is best *for you*. The more we rely on others, the less we trust ourselves—and the more we begin to live a life curated for approval, not alignment.

Most people give advice based on *their fears, regrets, and limitations*. They see the world through the lens of their past, not your future. Their doubts are not your destiny. Their wounds are not your path. Their beliefs are not your truth.

No one else knows you better than you. No one else carries the same passions, desires, or dreams as you. Others will tell you what *they* would do, but they cannot tell you what is *right for you*.

The cost of trying to make everyone around you happy is your own happiness.

But here's the good news: just because things *have* been a certain way doesn't mean they *have to stay* that way.

Frank Sonnenberg said, "Lessons in life will be repeated until they are learned." But how can we learn the lesson if no one shows us another way? We can't choose a new path until we realize there *is* one.

My hope for this guide is that it helps you to see life differently—to stop overthinking your decisions, to trust yourself again, and to find the courage to create a life that feels true to *you*.

Chapter 2

Why Do We Overthink?

"A decision made from fear is always the wrong decision."
—TONY ROBBINS

You don't overthink because something is wrong with you. You overthink because something *matters* to you.

Because you care. Because there's meaning wrapped in the moment. Because somewhere inside, you sense that this choice might shape your future—your identity, your safety, your connection to others.

But the root of overthinking is not care. It's fear.

Not the kind of fear that punches through your chest and announces itself in panic. It's the subtle kind. The kind that disguises itself as responsibility. The kind that whispers in the back of your mind: *What if you make the wrong choice? What if you can't handle what comes next? What if this is the thing that finally exposes you as not enough?*

If decisions were only logical, we wouldn't experience indecision. We'd weigh the pros and cons, make a choice, and move forward without giving it a second thought. But decisions aren't just calculations, they're mirrors. They show us who we think we are and who we're afraid we might be.

It's never just about *Which path should I take*. It's *What will it say about me if I make this choice? Will I still be loved, respected, safe, and successful?*

All overthinking—no matter the surface story—can be traced back to fear. Fear of failure. Fear of regret. Fear of disappointing others. Fear of not being who we think we should be.

And yet, overthinking doesn't mean something is wrong with your mind. It's evidence of a mind trying to protect you from these fears.

It builds mental simulations, plays out every scenario, and calculates every angle, not to find the truth—although it may feel this way—but to find control.

Control over pain. Control over loss. Control over how others see you.

But the allure of control is an illusion. Here's the paradox: the more we try to control, the more afraid we become and the less free we feel. It's like psychological quicksand—the more we struggle, the faster we sink into fear, self-doubt, and paralysis.

And so, the way out is not through grasping for control, but through acceptance. When you recognize and face fear, you don't give it power. You take it back. Because once you see fear clearly—not as truth, but as a pattern—it loosens its grip.

The moment you stop running from fear, it stops running your life.

Solving overthinking doesn't require another plan, another pro/con list, or another round of mental gymnastics. It requires your presence. Your grounded, clear-eyed willingness to feel what you've been avoiding.

This is the turning point.

Once you realize that all overthinking is just fear in disguise, you can stop battling every thought and simply address the root emotion.

And that's when a new possibility emerges: What if everything we've been taught about fear is backward? What if fear meant not that something was wrong but that you were on the verge of something right?

Think back—how many times was fear loudest right before you chose something that changed you for the better? The fear wasn't the problem, it was just your soul pointing to what you'd been searching for and what you were ready for all along.

What if fear was just a signal that something important is surfacing—a place within us still holding on to the illusion that our worth is conditional?

What if it was your soul letting you know what would help you grow the most?

Chapter 3

Your Focus Determines Your Decisions

"May your choices reflect your hopes, not your fears."
—NELSON MANDELA

Long before we had therapy, coaching, or neuroscience, humans understood something essential: that the mind contains many voices. Some bring clarity, and others bring confusion.

And that what determines our path is not which voice speaks the loudest but *which one we choose to listen to*. This isn't just a metaphor; it's how the mind works. Especially in moments of uncertainty, when fear and hope both speak at once.

There is a story often attributed to Cherokee tradition that depicts this universal human experience that has been passed down for generations. It lives on in moments like this—when fear and trust wrestle inside us for control.

An old man is teaching his grandson about life...

"A terrible fight is going on inside me," he tells the boy. "It is between two wolves. One is fear, envy, sorrow, regret, greed, and self-doubt. The other is joy, peace, love, hope, and confidence. The same fight is going on inside you—and inside every person, too."

The grandson thinks for a moment and asks, "Which wolf will win?"

The old man simply replies, "The one you feed."

Overcoming fear doesn't come from fighting it. The more you resist or avoid fear, the more you fan the flames of fear itself. Because resistance is still a form of attention, and attention is fuel. Trying to wrestle fear down is like throwing kindling on a blaze you're desperate to extinguish—it only makes it roar louder.

Fear is like fire: it doesn't die through struggle. It dies when you remove what keeps it alive.

What oxygen is to fire, your attention is to fear.

Remove the oxygen, and the flames go out.

Withdraw your attention from fear, and it begins to extinguish.

It doesn't need to be solved. It just needs to be seen for what it is.

You don't need to fight fear. You only need to *stop feeding it.*

The reality is that the emotion we make a decision from is the emotion we reinforce. This is because where our attention goes, energy flows. And where energy flows, things grow.

When we choose out of fear—fear of failure, rejection, or loss—we don't escape it; we perpetuate it.

When we focus on what we *don't* want, instead of avoiding it, we feed it. It grows until it overwhelms the decision-making process, keeping us trapped in a reactive, fight-or-flight state.

And yet, while it may be tempting to therefore think that the solution lies in minimizing emotion in general, we don't want to strip emotion from decision-making entirely. If we remove all emotion, we lose the "*good*" emotions that are crucial to decision-making as well: the hopes, the dreams, the desires, and the excitement.

This occurrence is why the goal isn't to eliminate emotion but to shift where we place our focus. So the decision becomes not about avoiding what we *don't* want but about moving toward what we *do* want.

When learning how to ski, the best instructors teach one simple rule: look where you want to go, not at the obstacles you wish to avoid. The moment you fixate on the trees, you veer toward them, and your likelihood of crashing into one increases. Not because they magically pull you in, but because your focus leads you there. **Your focus is a mental magnet.** It quietly draws you closer to whatever you give your attention to, whether it's the barriers you fear or the path you long to follow.

The same is true for decisions. When all your energy is spent trying to avoid the worst-case scenario, you don't move forward; you move *toward* the very thing you're trying to escape. You see only the barriers and lose sight of the way through.

The mind does not show us the world as it is—it shows us the world through the lens of what we expect to see. This experience is confirmation bias in action. When we fixate on fear, we train our minds to find more of it. When we believe something will go wrong, our brains search for proof, and we will always find evidence to support what we choose to believe. It filters reality to align with what we already expect, reinforcing the very patterns we're trying to escape.

This is why refocusing our attention isn't about ignoring reality; it's about *expanding our perception of it* so that we don't live a life formed only by fear and the negative. It's about fully accepting what is while seeing beyond it—recognizing new possibilities instead of unconsciously repeating old patterns.

By widening our lens, we don't reject the world as it is; we evolve beyond the limitations of how we once saw it. We give ourselves **permission to make decisions based on what we *want* instead of just avoiding what we fear.**

The same mechanism that keeps us stuck is the one that can set us free. Instead of focusing on the fear in a decision, focus on the possibility, and your mind will make choices that work to make your dreams a reality. Focus on what you want, and you will naturally begin to move toward it.

Make decisions based on how you *want* to feel rather than on what you're *afraid* to experience, and your life will be shaped by your dreams instead of your fears.

Attention is the architect of your reality.

The mind is fertile soil, and emotions are the seeds planted within it. Your attention is the water that brings them to life. Whatever you nourish—fear or love, doubt or confidence—will take root and grow. The mind does not discriminate; it breeds what you feed it.

If you make decisions to avoid fear, you are watering the weeds of worry, allowing them to spread and take over. But if you make decisions to cultivate peace, love, and joy, you are tending to a garden of growth and expansion, where each decision plants the future you want to live in.

The soil does not choose what grows. *You do.*

Chapter 4

Where Our Best Decisions Come From

"The best decisions aren't made with your mind, but with your Instinct."

—LIONEL MESSI

Recall a decision that profoundly changed your life for the better. Maybe it was moving to a new city, changing careers, pursuing a passion, or starting/ending a relationship. Choosing to take care of your health. Starting a business or writing a book.

When you made the decision, was it purely logical, or was there something deeper at play? Did you weigh every opinion, seeking external validation, or did you trust yourself despite the uncertainty? Was it driven by fear and safety, or did it feel like stepping into something bigger than yourself? Did you make it to meet expectations, or did it come from a sense of alignment and inner truth?

More likely than not, this life-altering decision wasn't the safest, most rational, most socially acceptable choice.

It didn't come from the part of you obsessed with control, certainty, and minimizing risk. It came from focusing on your hopes and dreams, from what you imagined your life could be. It came from somewhere beyond opinions, beyond fear, beyond logic—it came from *you.*

Not the version of you conditioned to conform. Not the version of you that prioritizes security over growth. But the *real* you. The one that knows, deep down, that growth—not comfort—is the path to a life of meaning, peace, and fulfillment.

Your best decisions don't come from the mind that hesitates, overthinks, and asks, *What will other people think of me? What if it doesn't work out?*

They come from the part of you that feels, *What is my heart saying I'm meant to do? What would I choose if I weren't afraid? What feels undeniably right, even if it doesn't make sense yet? What am I unexplainably pulled toward?*

This is your intuition speaking, and it is who you truly are—the part of you that sees beyond fear and into possibility. The part of you that recognizes that real security comes not from playing small but from stepping fully into alignment with who you were meant to be.

The only filter that matters when making choices is this:

Will it contract who you are or expand who you're becoming?

Because the truth is, the best decisions of your life will never be found in the logic of the mind. They will be felt in the *knowing* of your heart.

This doesn't mean you should ignore knowledge or act without understanding. Gathering information matters, but only to the point where it brings you greater clarity, not greater confusion. There's a moment when seeking more shifts from empowering you to paralyzing you. You'll know you've reached that point when additional thinking doesn't create more certainty but instead deepens your confusion and doubt. That's when it's time to stop asking your mind and start trusting what you already know deep down.

Your best decisions come from trusting yourself. From listening to that still, small voice inside—the one only *you* can hear. From following what you *know* to be true, even when it doesn't make sense to others. From choosing your heart over your fear, and alignment over approval.

Not because it keeps you safe. But because it sets you *free*.

Chapter 5

But What If I Make the Wrong Decision by Trusting Myself?

"Sometimes you make the right decision,
sometimes you make the decision right."

—PHIL MCGRAW

There is an ancient Chinese story from the second century BCE that beautifully illustrates why we shouldn't rush to label events as ultimately "good" or "bad" and reveals the philosophical truth that all situations are constantly evolving.

The Story of the Wise Farmer

There was once an old farmer who lived on the border of an ancient kingdom. He was known not for his wealth or his status but for the way he responded to life, as if he saw something the rest of the village missed.

One day, his only horse broke free and ran away across the hills.

The neighbors rushed over: "What terrible news! This is such bad luck."

The old farmer just said, "Maybe. We'll see."

A few weeks later, the horse returned, and behind it trailed a group of wild stallions.

Now the neighbors came running again.

"What incredible luck! You've multiplied your fortune!"

Again, the old farmer said, "Maybe. We'll see."

His son, young and full of fire, tried to tame one of the new horses. But the horse bucked and threw him hard to the ground.

His leg was badly broken.

The neighbors shook their heads. "What a tragedy. Your poor son."

The old farmer only said, "Maybe. We'll see."

Months passed, and the kingdom fell into war. Soldiers came to draft every able-bodied young man.

But the farmer's son was spared because his broken leg made him unfit for battle.

> Most of the other young men never returned home.

> The villagers were quiet this time.

We're taught to label things as *right* or *wrong*, *good* or *bad*, *successes* or *failures*—as if life is that absolute. But the truth is: Outcomes are rarely what we expect, and we don't know enough to judge all that will come from one decision.

At the moment when you make a decision, it is too soon to tell all the effects it will have. Some will be good, some will be bad, and most will be impossible to predict. A decision you regret today might be the very thing that leads to a discovery tomorrow. A path that feels unclear or difficult might be clearing away something that wasn't serving you.

Most events in life aren't entirely good or bad—they often hold the potential for both, depending on how we relate to them.

Take a volcanic eruption, for example. To those nearby, it may bring destruction, loss, and upheaval. But over time, that same eruption enriches the soil, creating some of the most fertile land on earth. Entire ecosystems return, more vibrant than before.

So is the eruption a tragedy or a necessity? The event itself doesn't decide that; we do. To the earth, it isn't good or bad; it simply is. It's a process, not a judgment. It's not the eruption that carries meaning; but the label we give it and the narrative we create about it in our minds.

And in that way, it reflects a larger truth: all events are inherently neutral. *We* are the ones who assign meaning, and the label we give determines how we feel about a situation. This isn't meant to dismiss the reality of pain. There are countless deeply difficult, heartbreaking, tragic events in this world. But it's important to recognize that even in those moments, our labels can either weigh us down or help us rise.

This is how it is with decisions, too. Think back to a decision you consider "good." Did it only bring positive outcomes? Or did it come with a cost? A door closed, a connection altered, a part of you quietly wondering, even now, about a different path.

Now recall a decision you labeled "bad." Did it only lead to regret? Or did it push you to grow, reveal your strengths, or guide you to something better that you couldn't have planned?

Most decisions lead to a mix of outcomes—some expected, some not. Yet we often judge the decision itself as absolutely good or bad based solely on how the story has played out *so far*.

Even with the most thoughtful, carefully planned decisions, we never have full control over how they turn out. Which means that our power lies not in whether the decision works out exactly the way we hoped but in how we respond.

The truth is that how we feel about a decision is shaped much less by the outcome itself than by the meaning we assign to it.

Sometimes, the most powerful shift begins with simply releasing the story you've been telling yourself. Letting go of the negative response—*"this shouldn't have happened," "this was wrong"*—doesn't mean denying the pain. It means we stop adding to it with the weight of judgment.

When you're not acting from harm, there are no inherently "wrong" decisions.

There are no perfect paths, just as there are no perfect decisions. Only choices that limit or expand who you are. Only decisions that are unaligned or aligned with who you are becoming.

And the beautiful part is: You can *feel* the difference. Your body knows. Your breath knows.

When you make decisions out of fear, anxiety, or the need for approval, something inside you tightens. That tightening is often a sign that you're making decisions from the *outside in*—letting outcomes, expectations, or other people's opinions dictate your direction. And when you do that, you place your ability to find peace in the hands of things entirely beyond your control.

But when you make choices from the *inside out*—guided by alignment, intuition, and your quiet knowing—something softens and expands. Even if it's uncomfortable or uncertain, there's a sense of lightness, of truth, of coming home to yourself. You stop chasing the "right" outcome and start honoring what's *right for you*.

The more we ground our decisions in inner truth, the more we begin to realize: **There are no failures, only**

invitations to grow. No path is wasted. Every decision offers something we need, whether it's clarity, healing, strength, or the reminder to listen more closely next time.

When growth becomes the goal, fear begins to dissolve. In doing so, you release the pressure to choose the perfect path and become the person who can walk any path with presence, courage, and peace.

This is where real confidence is born—not from trying to *control* the future, but from knowing that you can *weather any* future.

When your peace is rooted in how you meet life—not in what life gives you—you begin to trust something far more powerful than control.

You begin to trust your ability to stay centered in uncertainty. To adapt, respond, and evolve.

You stop spiraling when plans fall apart.

You stop second-guessing every step.

You still feel the fear, but it no longer decides for you. Discomfort isn't a problem to solve; it's a signal you're on the right path. It's a sign not of weakness but of growth. And it's proof that you're no longer avoiding who you're meant to become.

It's a sign that you are a person who trusts that even if things go sideways, you'll find your way back. Not because the path is perfect, but because you know how to listen.

Not because everything goes right, but because *you no longer need it to.*

Think of life as a compass.

You don't need to know every twist and turn to get to your destination. You only need to take the next step and trust that your inner guidance will lead you from there. And if you take a detour, the compass doesn't scold you. It doesn't criticize, shame, or call you foolish for taking a wrong turn. It simply points you north so you can find your way back again. You don't need to panic if you make a "wrong turn"; you can always course correct.

Your inner guidance never makes you question your worth.

We are the ones who do.

Life doesn't demand perfection.

We are the ones who do.

Your inner compass—your intuition, your deeper knowing—only ever wants to guide you to where you're meant to be. No matter how many turns it takes.

And truthfully, there is no path without obstacles.

No road without bumps.

No journey without unexpected delays.

So the goal isn't to pick the perfect path. It's to become the person who trusts themselves enough to navigate *any* path. Some paths will be smoother. Some will be rougher. Others are more scenic. But all of them will take you where you're meant to go—as long as you keep choosing what feels true to you.

And remember, no decision is final. You're not locked into any one path forever.

You're allowed to change. To grow. To *outgrow* who you've been and choose a version of yourself that feels more alive, more free, more whole.

You don't have to get every decision right to get there. You're going to make mistakes no matter what. But when you make decisions that feel true to you, you reclaim not just your power, but your peace.

And when you listen to your inner voice, you gain something far greater than just options—you gain freedom, including the freedom to make mistakes.

There is no learning without mistakes.

No growth without discomfort.

No enlightenment without suffering.

They're all sides of the same coin.

If it's true that you can't avoid the inevitable obstacles of life no matter which path you choose, you may as well live a life of liberation on your terms.

You've spent your life trying to avoid the wrong choice. But what if the only mistake was believing you weren't strong enough to navigate whatever life has in store?

Chapter 6

What If My Decision Upsets Someone I Care About?

"One of the greatest regrets in life is being what others would want you to be, rather than being yourself."

—SHANNON L. ALDER

Sometimes, your decisions will upset others. There is always someone who will disagree and disapprove of what you choose to do with your life. But that doesn't necessarily mean you made the wrong choice—it may simply mean that you're choosing to honor your truth instead of their expectations. And for some people, that will feel uncomfortable, especially if they've become accustomed to your self-abandonment.

We're often conditioned—through culture, family, work, or even friends—to believe that being a "good" person means keeping the peace, minimizing conflict, and making sure others feel okay, even if it costs us our peace. We mistake approval for happiness, thinking that if we just make the "right" choice in the eyes of others, we will finally feel whole.

But no amount of outside validation will ever make you feel like you're enough. And over time, that constant pleasing begins to hollow us out. It disconnects us from ourselves and places our sense of self-worth in the hands of other people's approval.

When you prioritize other people's opinions and desires over your truth, you begin to lose sight of who you are. You become an echo of others' expectations, an empty vessel hoping to be filled with their approval.

But here's the truth most of us were never taught:

Your peace does not need to be sacrificed for someone else's comfort.

And someone else's comfort should never come at the expense of your growth, your joy, or your sense of alignment.

Their reaction is not your responsibility—but your integrity is.

And the real question is not "What if they're upset?" but rather: "What is more important—your peace or their approval?"

The best thing you can ask from others is their support, not their validation. Their perspective, not their permission.

If someone makes you feel guilty for choosing what is true and life-giving for you—if they are upset that you are choosing joy, growth, or rest—you have to gently ask yourself:

Do they truly want me to be happy, or do they want me to keep them happy at the cost of my happiness?

It's easy to confuse guilt with wrongdoing. But feeling guilty is often just an echo of old conditioning, not proof that you've made a mistake. Especially when your decision isn't causing harm but simply disappointing someone who benefits from your self-sacrifice.

People who love you *conditionally* will want you to choose them, even if it means abandoning yourself.

People who love you *unconditionally* will want you to choose what makes you come alive—even if it challenges them, even if it changes the relationship, even if it means letting go of their idea of who they thought you were.

This doesn't mean you should cut people off or harden your heart. It doesn't mean you should burn bridges and justify it as empowerment. It means you can learn to hold compassion and boundaries at the same time. You can stay kind while staying true to yourself. You can remain loving while being honest about what no longer works.

At the end of the day, relationships will change as you do. Some may fall away—not because you were too much, but because you stopped being too little.

If that happens, it's not a loss. It's a gentle, purposeful pruning of your life that releases what no longer serves you. A spiritual shedding of who you once were, so that you can make space for who you're becoming.

And if that makes someone angry, it doesn't mean something is wrong with you. Anger is often grief in disguise—a mourning for the version of you they were attached to, the version who said yes when you meant no. And that grief may come out as blame, guilt, or withdrawal.

You can honor their grief without collapsing into it.

You can hold space for their pain without sacrificing your becoming.

You're allowed to keep growing, even if they don't understand yet.

And you can love them through their process without losing yourself in it.

The most loving thing you can do in those moments is to reassure them that your love for them hasn't disappeared. It's just evolving. It may no longer look the way they expected, but it can still be real. It can still be kind. It can still be love.

You can tend to their feelings, explaining your decision and offering emotional support as you help them work through their reaction. But you can do this without letting their emotions determine or override your decisions.

Trying to keep everyone happy is a subconscious attempt to control what you cannot. And it's one of the surest ways to suffer because it keeps your sense of self-worth tied to other people's emotional states, which you were never meant to carry.

The people who truly love you—*not just who you've been for them, but who you are in your essence*—will want you to feel whole. Not just agreeable. Not just convenient. But fulfilled, expressed, and free.

Sometimes, the most loving thing you can do for someone else is to stop living your life to make them happy—because it gives them permission to do the same. And sometimes, the most loving thing you can do for yourself is to let go of the version of you who lived in fear of disappointing others.

True love doesn't trap you in obligation.

It invites you into freedom.

And freedom will often ask you to disappoint others so that you no longer disappoint yourself.

Chapter 7

So How Do We Actually Make Better Decisions?

"Decision is a risk rooted in the courage of being free."
—PAUL TILLICH

As we explored earlier, the way we feel about our decisions—before, during, and after making them—is shaped by *how* we make them. When we choose from fear—trying to avoid regret, loss, or judgment—we only end up strengthening the very fear we hoped to escape.

But when we shift our focus from what we *don't* want to what we *do* want to experience, when we move from fear to trust, from avoidance to alignment, something subtle but profound begins to change. We stop reacting and we start creating.

Because our experience of reality is not something we passively observe. It's something we actively shape. It is not fixed; it's *fluid*. Every choice is a brushstroke on the canvas of our existence, and the more we choose from fear, the more we paint in the colors of limitation.

But the opposite is also true.

There are deeper voices that call to us—quietly, consistently—beneath all the noise: a desire for peace, a sense of truth, the pull to grow, and the longing to live with more love and possibility.

We don't often name them. We rarely prioritize them. But when we choose from these places, we begin to live differently.

They're not just ideas but ways of being we long for and are meant to live from.

This type of decision is what we'll call an *actualized decision*.

An actualized decision is a choice made not from fear, pressure, or the need for approval, but from self-trust, alignment, presence, and love.

Sometimes, the most aligned decision feels scary—not because it's wrong, but because it invites you to outgrow the limits you once needed to feel safe.

It doesn't guarantee success, but it brings peace in the midst of uncertainty.

The best decisions aren't made from stress and panic. They're made when you feel safe, centered, and present. Counterintuitively, by letting go of our attachment to outcomes, we give ourselves the greatest chance of making the best decision possible.

Psychologist Abraham Maslow once described a hierarchy of human needs, from the most basic (like food and safety) to the highest: self-actualization—the full expression of our potential and truest self. A state in which your thoughts, actions, and values begin to reflect who you truly are—beneath fear, conditioning, or external expectation.

An actualized decision emerges from that same place.

The Dimensions of an Actualized Decision

If we stop choosing from fear, we need a different guide to replace it. And that's where most people get stuck because we were never taught how to recognize more than a *safe* decision. But to make this shift, we need to learn to recognize how to make an *aligned* one.

Instead of asking, *"What's the right choice?"*

We need to ask: **"What kind of life do I want to create with this choice?"**

And from that place, we begin choosing with intention.

The deeper experiences we long for—peace, alignment, growth, and abundance—aren't just abstract ideals. They are the foundation of a new way of choosing: what we'll call the four dimensions of an *actualized decision*.

To make them easy to remember, they form the acronym **SAGE:**

▷ **Serenity**—Which choice will give me the deepest peace?
▷ **Alignment**—Which choice aligns with who I want to become?
▷ **Growth**—Which choice expands me the most?

▷ **Emotion**—Which choice is driven by love and abundance rather than fear?

This isn't a checklist to complete. It's a compass, one that helps you stay aligned and gently brings you back when you've strayed. Let it guide you, not to the "right" answer, but to the one that aligns with who you're here to become.

And like any true compass, it doesn't criticize when you take a wrong turn. It doesn't shame you for getting lost or punish you for changing course. It simply recalibrates—quietly, patiently—offering you a new way forward from exactly where you are.

Even when the road is unclear, even when you can't see what's ahead, this compass remains. It doesn't demand perfection.

It offers presence.

And the more you learn to trust it, the more you realize: you were never off track.

Never behind. Never broken.

Just momentarily disconnected from your own knowing. Because there's peace in remembering there is no perfect path.

And when you step back and look at the map of your life, you'll see that every turn—every detour, every delay, every decision—was leading you to the same place all along:

Back home to yourself.

Chapter 8

The TRUST Decision-Making Framework

"Your heart knows the way. Run in that direction."
—RUMI

Now that you understand the philosophy of making decisions, let's distill it into a simple, practical, and memorable framework you can use every day. The TRUST Decision-Making Framework is a five-step practice designed to help you break through overthinking and make actualized decisions that are aligned with who you are and who you're becoming. This framework is the step-by-step process for how we apply SAGE to our daily decisions, no matter how big or small. When you find yourself spiraling in indecision, stuck in a loop of what-ifs and worst-case scenarios, pause, breathe, and walk yourself through this process.

The TRUST Framework isn't meant to give you the "right" answer. It's intended to help you remember that *you already know*: that knowledge has just been buried beneath fear, noise, and pressure. It's designed to help you leave behind the fear and anxiety of overthinking and make decisions from a place of peace and intuition.

Overthinking doesn't mean something is wrong with you. It means your nervous system is overwhelmed and your mind; is trying to protect you the only way it knows how—by reaching for control. But attempting to control what we cannot doesn't create clarity; it creates overwhelm. And so this framework isn't about fighting the mind; it's about gently redirecting it toward something deeper: your truth.

As you go through each step, answer the questions as honestly and compassionately as you can. Suspend judgment—of yourself, your circumstances, and your uncertainty. Judgment doesn't bring clarity; it only keeps you stuck in fear.

By the end of this process, you won't just have an answer. You'll have something far more powerful: a decision that feels *true.* One that comes not from fear or people-pleasing but from clarity, alignment, and trust in yourself.

T—Take Five Deep Breaths

Before anything else, come home to your body. Overthinking is often a sign that you're stuck in your head, disconnected from your inner wisdom.

Taking five deep, intentional breaths activates your parasympathetic nervous system, grounds you in the present moment, and begins to calm the storm. It's the first step in shifting from reaction to clarity—from fear to truth.

You don't make great decisions in a panic. You make them when you feel safe, centered, and present.

PRACTICE:
- ▷ Regulate the nervous system by taking five slow, deep breaths.
- ▷ Try the two-to-one breathing technique: inhale for four seconds, and exhale for eight.

R—Reveal the Root Decision

When we're overwhelmed, we often lose sight of the actual decision we're trying to make. Our minds spiral into endless hypotheticals, and the choice balloons until it becomes something much larger than the actual decision at hand.

Instead of getting lost in the noise, zoom in: *What is the real decision here?*

Don't confuse the symptoms with the cause. For example, if you're considering leaving your job, your mind might be preoccupied with what your boss will think, whether your coworkers will be disappointed, or if you'll find another job in time. But all of that is just noise.

Strip it back. The root decision is: *Do I stay, or do I go?* Naming the real decision brings relief and is the first step to clarity. Simplicity cuts through confusion.

PRACTICE:
- ▷ State the decision you are facing in one clear sentence. Don't include the possible outcomes or emotions, just the decision at hand *(e.g., "Stay in this job or leave?")*.
- ▷ What event prompted this decision *(e.g., "My boss criticized my work")?*

U—Uncover the Fear and the Cost of Listening to It

At the root of overthinking is fear. Not the loud kind that screams danger, but the quieter kind that disguises itself in responsibility, doubt, and control. To move past it, we first have to name it.

What fear is this decision bringing up? What are you afraid it will mean if you choose wrong? Naming fear doesn't give it power—it reclaims your own. Once you see fear clearly, it begins to loosen its hold. And when you understand why you overthink, letting go becomes natural.

But fear of a bad outcome isn't the only thing that paralyzes us. It's the meaning we attach to the outcome that makes the fear so heavy. It's not just, *"I might fail."* It's, *"If I fail, it will mean I'm not good enough."* The story we tell ourselves is what traps us. If we can spot the story—not as truth but as a habit that no longer serves us—we can begin to dissolve it.

But stories that have lived inside us for years aren't dismantled by logic alone. Their roots go deep, and they hold on until we recognize the real cost of believing them. Fear demands a high price: our peace, our time, our confidence, our dreams. Ask yourself: What has fear already taken from me? If I keep listening to it, where will I be a year from now? Five years? Ten?

We are often more moved by the pain of what we're losing than the promise of what we could gain. When you see clearly what fear has already taken—and what it will continue to take—you find a deeper kind of courage. A strength that rises not because you're fearless but because you're no longer willing to trade your life for the illusion of safety.

At some point, the cost of playing it safe becomes greater than the risk of being true to yourself—and that is a decision not of the mind but of the soul.

PRACTICE:
  ▷ What are you afraid might happen if you choose wrong? What do you worry that choosing wrong would mean about you *(e.g., "I'll fail," "I'm not good enough")?*
  ▷ What is this fear costing you *(e.g., "Constantly seeking validation is eroding my self-confidence")?*

S—Shift from Fear to Intuition

Here's where everything changes.

If all fear vanished—if every voice of doubt and expectation and judgment disappeared—*what would you choose?*

What feels most expansive?

Shift your focus to the emotions you wish to cultivate. What possibility is most exciting to you? What choice contains more peace, freedom, love, or joy?

Let your intuition speak. Let it lead. Listen to your inner

voice, not the voices of others—even if they're well-intentioned. This is how you move from outside-in decision-making to inside-out. From reaction to alignment. From contraction to expansion.

You'll often feel this as a subtle shift—not fireworks, but a breath of relief. A loosening in the chest. A softening in your jaw. A feeling of being less at war with yourself.

Remember that there are inherently no good or bad, right or wrong decisions. Only ones that are aligned or unaligned with who you are. Your future is determined much less by the outcome than by your response to it. True confidence comes not from trying to control what happens but from trusting you can navigate whatever happens.

When in doubt, ask: *Which decision feels rooted in fear? Which one feels rooted in love and expansion?*

PRACTICE:

> ▷ Using the principles of SAGE, which choice will bring the most long-term peace, alignment, and growth—even if it feels scary to choose?
> ▷ Suspend judgment and give yourself permission to consider this choice an actual possibility. How would it feel to choose this option?
> ▷ If you release your attachment to outcomes and trust you can navigate whatever happens, what is your intuition telling you to choose?
> ▷ Write down your actualized decision.

T—Take the Smallest Possible Action

We often freeze, not because the decision is wrong, but because it feels too big, too scary to confront.

The antidote? Shrink it.

Ask yourself: *What is the smallest possible step I can take right now? One that's so doable it feels almost silly not to do it.*

Not making the whole career change, just updating your resume.

Not writing the whole book, just starting the first sentence.

Not completing the full workout, just showing up at the gym.

The goal isn't to finish. It's to begin.

Because once you move, you're no longer stuck; you're becoming.

PRACTICE:

▷ What's the first small step you can take that will make this choice a reality?

TRUST Decision-Making Framework

1. Take Five Deep Breaths
   ▷ Regulate the nervous system by taking five slow, deep breaths. Try the two-to-one breathing technique: inhale for four seconds, and exhale for eight.

2. Reveal the Root Decision
   ▷ State the decision you are facing in one clear sentence. Don't include the possible outcomes or emotions, just the decision at hand.
   ▷ What event prompted this decision?

3. Uncover the Fear & Its Cost
   ▷ What are you afraid might happen if you choose wrong? What do you worry that choosing wrong would mean about you?
   ▷ What is this fear costing you?

4. Shift from Fear to Intuition
   ▷ Using the principles of SAGE, which choice will bring the most long-term peace, alignment, and growth—even if it feels scary to choose?
   ▷ Suspend judgment and give yourself permission to consider this choice an actual possibility. How would it feel to choose this option?
   ▷ If you release your attachment to outcomes and trust you can navigate whatever happens, what is your intuition telling you to choose?
   ▷ Write down your actualized decision.

5. Take the Smallest Possible Action
   ▷ What's the first small step you can take that will make this choice a reality?

Chapter 9

Conclusion:
A New Perspective

"Always go with the choice that scares you the most, because that's the one that is going to require the most from you. Do you really want to look back on your life and see how wonderful it could have been had you not been afraid to live it?"

—CAROLINE MYSS

The root of overthinking is fear—fear of making the "wrong" choice, of failing, of being exposed as a fraud, of judgment, of not being enough. And the more attention we give that fear, the more real it becomes.

Because reality is not fixed; it's created. Created by where we place our focus, what we believe, and what we feed with our attention.

We struggle with indecision not because of the decision itself but because of the emotional weight we attach to it—the belief that one wrong move could unravel everything.

The mind craves certainty. It craves safety.

But life offers neither guarantee nor control, only opportunity.

It offers something more sacred: *choice.*

The freedom to begin again. The power to create what's next.

So the work isn't to eliminate fear.

It's to stop letting it choose for you.

Fear is not a stop sign but an invitation. It does not warn you of danger; it signals where the most meaningful growth lies. Fear is not the enemy; it's a guide. It arises not to hold you back but to point you toward what matters most. If it didn't mean something, you wouldn't feel it.

The paradox of fear is that avoiding it perpetuates it. Confronting it dissolves it. Avoiding fear means you are also avoiding everything you want. Fear stands between you and the life you desire—not as a wall, but as a test. It is not in the way; it *is* the way. The price of your dreams is fear. Nothing else.

Happiness isn't the result of self-abandonment. And personal freedom isn't something granted through the permission of others. The moment you stop searching for the "right" choice and start trusting the one that already feels right, the weight begins to lift. Not because the decision itself becomes easier, but because you stop resisting what you already know.

Those who truly love you want your authentic happiness, not your compliance. The greatest gift you can offer them is not your sacrifice but your flourishing. Perhaps, then, the bravest decision is not self-sacrifice but self-trust.

Chapter 10

The Threshold Before You

"We are the creative force of our life, and through our own decisions rather than our conditions, if we carefully learn to do certain things, we can accomplish those goals."

—STEPHEN COVEY

You've already begun to change.

Maybe quietly. Subtly. In ways even you didn't expect. But it's unmistakable now.

The way you view indecision, the weight you've carried, the patterns you couldn't quite name—all now brought into light.

This new perspective isn't just insight; it's a transformation in motion.

You've seen the truth: that the way you've been making decisions is no longer working—not because you're broken, but because you've outgrown it. You now hold a new lens—and a new language—for choosing.

Because once you see through the lens of truth, you can't unsee it. Once you remember that you are allowed to trust yourself, you can't go back to abandoning yourself in the same way.

You've crossed a threshold and there's no uncrossing it.

But information alone doesn't change your life. Integration does.

Which is why what comes next is about embodiment. About translating what's awakened inside you into the way you move through the world. Not perfectly, but intentionally. Not for others, but finally for yourself.

The pages ahead aren't just exercises. They're your invitation to begin again—not as the person you've had to be, but as the person you're finally ready to become.

Here's what's next:

▷ **Decision-Making Principles**
Your internal compass. A distilled map of the truths you've uncovered—so that you never lose your way when old habits try to pull you back.

▷ **Discovering Yourself as a Decision-Maker**
Powerful prompts to help you uncover how you've been making choices and what it's been costing you and transform the way you choose.

▷ **Practicing TRUST**
Step-by-step guidance to help in moments where you're struggling with indecision—so you can stop spiraling, start choosing, and begin living in alignment.

▷ **Tiny Acts of Self-Trust**

Simple, playful exercises to rewire how you relate to choice—training your nervous system to respond not with fear but with clarity and confidence.

The next sections discuss how the theory becomes lived wisdom. Through practice.

The life you've longed for is no longer a distant idea. It's here, asking for your participation.

This is where it becomes real.

Now is your chance to build a life that reflects it.

Not a life built on approval.

Not a life built on fear.

But a life that feels like *home* in your soul.

This isn't just a new chapter.

It's a rediscovery of who you truly are.

You've abandoned yourself for far too long.

Now it's time to trust yourself again.

Chapter 11

Guide to Using This Book Most Effectively

When you feel lost or disconnected from clarity, return to the *Decision-Making Principles.* It's your compass—a distilled map of the deepest truths in this book. Let it center you.

When you're struggling with indecision, walk through the *TRUST exercise.* It's designed to help you move from fear to clarity, from spiraling thoughts to grounded alignment.

When you're ready to understand the patterns behind your choices, spend time in the *Discovering Yourself as a Decision-Maker* section. It will help you uncover what's been shaping your decisions and what you want to shift moving forward.

When you want to playfully practice trusting yourself in everyday moments, choose a challenge from *Tiny Acts of Self-Trust.* These low-stakes invitations will help you embody what you've learned in ways that are fun, freeing, and surprisingly powerful.

Suggested Practice

You don't need to follow a fixed sequence, but if you want to experience the deepest shifts this book can offer, following this simple plan can help you integrate the insights into your daily life and create real, lasting change:

▷ **Every time you find yourself overthinking a decision:**
Review the *Decision-Making Principles* and complete the *TRUST exercise* to move from confusion to clarity.

▷ **Once a day:**
Answer a prompt from *Discovering Yourself as a Decision-Maker* to better understand how you make decisions and begin transforming the way you choose.

▷ **Once a week:**
Complete a *Tiny Act of Self-Trust* to gently stretch your courage and remind yourself that you can trust your inner guidance—one small choice at a time.

Scan the QR code below to download printable versions of all the key frameworks, principles, and decision-making tools from this book.

Chapter 12

Decision-Making Principles

This is a collection of the most powerful, perspective-shifting truths in this book. These aren't just concepts to understand; they are waypoints to guide you. Lenses to see differently. Anchors to return to. Reminders of the deeper wisdom you already carry.

Read through them slowly—not just with your mind, but with your heart. Notice what resonates. What expands your perspective or gently shifts the way you think? What feels like truth?

Let each principle be more than advice. Let it be a mirror reflecting the version of you that already knows what to do when you tune into yourself. Come back to this page whenever you feel uncertain. Not to find the "right" answer but to realign with who you are becoming. The version of you who trusts yourself. Who chooses from love, not fear. Who makes decisions not to avoid life but to fully live it.

Fear & Protection

1. The root of overthinking is fear.
2. You're not stuck in indecision because you don't know what to do. You're stuck because you're afraid of what you will lose if you choose wrong.
3. Fear is an indication not that something is wrong but that you are on the verge of something right.
4. Fear is not a stop sign—it's a compass pointing toward what matters most.
5. Fear is not in the way. It is the way.
6. Fear and desire are two sides of the same coin. On the other side of fear is everything you're looking for in life.
7. Fear no longer controls you the moment you decide that your peace and growth matter more than avoiding what you're afraid of.
8. Every decision is either a step into fear or a step into freedom.

Intuition & Inner Knowing

9. The mind thinks, but intuition knows.
10. The mind will convince you that you don't know what to choose even though your intuition always does.
11. The best decisions of your life will never be found in the logic of the mind. They will be felt in the intuitive knowing of your heart.

12. The clarity you seek doesn't come before making a decision. It comes from making a decision.
13. No one else has to understand your decision for it to be right for you.
14. Give yourself the permission you keep waiting for others to give you.

Growth, Alignment & Choice

15. One of the greatest powers we possess is choice.
16. There are no inherently right, wrong, or perfect decisions—only ones that are aligned or unaligned.
17. At the heart of every decision is this question: Will this contract who you are or expand who you're becoming?
18. The best decision is the one that brings the most long-term peace, alignment, and growth.
19. The purpose of life is not to get it right but to grow. The weight of the decision lifts when you realize: No matter what you choose, you're going to grow. To create a life you love, make decisions based on what you want instead of making decisions to avoid what you fear.
20. No decision is final. You can always choose again.

Self-Trust & Emotional Freedom

21. If peace requires self-betrayal, it's not peace—it's people-pleasing.
22. The people who truly love you won't need you to abandon yourself to be loved by them.
23. Most advice is other people telling you what they would do—but they cannot tell you what's right for you.
24. Your focus determines your decisions.
25. Your focus is a mental magnet. What you place your attention on is what you attract more of in your life.
26. The emotion you make a decision from is the emotion you reinforce.
27. Attention is the architect of your reality.
28. No outcome is absolutely good or bad. Every outcome contains both positive and negative consequences.
29. We have power over *how* we make decisions but not their outcomes. Who you are is determined not by what happens but by how you respond to it.
30. Peace and confidence do not come from trying to control outcomes. They come from trusting that you will be able to navigate any outcome.
31. Ultimately, it's not the outcome that defines your path. It's your response that shapes your life.

"Every decision brings with it some good, some bad, some lessons, and some luck. The only thing that's for sure is that indecision steals many years from many people who wind up wishing they'd just had the courage to leap."

—DOE ZANTAMATA

II.

Discovering Yourself as a Decision-Maker

Guided Reflections to Understand
and Transform How You Choose

*"At any given moment we have
two options: to step forward into
growth or to step back into safety."*

—ABRAHAM MASLOW

Part 1: Self-Discovery

Without awareness, nothing can change. With it, everything can. This section isn't about judging your patterns; it's about seeing them. Your decision-making has been shaped by experiences, beliefs, and fears, often without your awareness. The goal isn't to fix anything immediately but to simply notice what's been guiding you.

There are **no right or wrong answers here.** Take your time, there's no rush. Approach this with curiosity, as if discovering yourself for the first time. Awareness is the first step in change. Be kind to yourself as you go through the questions. These aren't meant to overwhelm you but to help uncover the hidden forces influencing your decisions.

What you uncover may surprise you, but that's not a problem; it's a doorway. The more honest you are, the more freeing this will be. By the end, you'll see yourself—and your decisions—in a whole new light.

Before you complete the next section, respond to the following question to help you begin reflecting on your decision-making:

What are some decisions you've made recently that you found yourself overthinking? It doesn't matter if the outcome of these decisions was good or bad, what matters is how the process felt. Write them down, and they may be helpful memories to reference when answering the following questions.

Chapter 13

Revealing the Hidden Patterns

Bringing awareness to your current decision-making process.

How would you describe yourself as a decision-maker? How does decision-making typically go for you?

_____

_____

_____

_____

_____

_____

How much do you overthink decisions?

NOT AT ALL   INTENSELY

(1)   (2)   (3)   (4)   (5)

What percentage of your decisions would you say you overthink?

NONE   ALL

(1)   (2)   (3)   (4)   (5)

Which kinds of decisions tend to trigger overthinking and which don't?

D O	DON'T

Why do you think that is?

What does overthinking feel like for you? (Note physical and psychological symptoms.)

PHYSICAL   PSYCHOLOGICAL

What patterns do you   BEFORE
notice in how you tend
to feel and react before,
during, and after making
a hard decision?

DURING   AFTER

If someone close to you observed your decision-making, what would they see you struggling with?

Do you feel that you make better decisions when you overthink? Why or why not?

When you're struggling to make a decision, what does it usually take for you to finally make it? What gets you past the overthinking?

What would you like to change about your decision-making?

Chapter 14

The Role of Emotions

Understanding how our emotions impact our decision-making more than we might realize.

What emotions feel most present when you're making difficult decisions? Make sure to note all emotions: positive, negative, in-between.

Do you make decisions based more on fear or growth?

FEAR   GROWTH

(1)   (2)   (3)   (4)   (5)

Why do you think that is?

How often is fear a part of your decision-making process?

NEVER   ALWAYS

(1)   (2)   (3)   (4)   (5)

What does this fear feel like in your mind and body?

MIND   BODY

How do you feel when you make decisions from a place of
fear? During the decision? After?

What are your biggest fears when making decisions?

Where do you think these fears come from? Where else do they show up in your life?

FEAR	ORIGIN	WHERE IT APPEARS

Chapter 15

The Influence of
External Pressure

*Uncovering how external opinions
and forces affect our decisions.*

Whose approval do you seek—consciously or unconsciously—
when making choices? Why do you want their validation?

What do you believe will happen if you disappoint someone
with your decision?

What do you think it would mean about you if you disappointed someone you cared about?

If a choice feels deeply right but might upset someone you care about, what tends to carry more weight: their comfort or your peace?

THEIR COMFORT   YOUR PEACE

(1)   (2)   (3)   (4)   (5)

Why do you think that is?

If disappointing them meant peace for you, would you allow it?

Where do you think this urge to please and not disappoint others comes from? Do you remember when you first felt it?

Recognizing Judgment and Narratives

Revealing the internalized stories that have been shaping your choices.

What questions tend to run through your mind when you're unsure of what to choose in a decision? Do they bring clarity or more confusion?

_____

_____

_____

_____

_____

What do you believe you must avoid at all costs when making a decision? What emotions or outcomes feel intolerable? Why do you think that is?

_____

_____

_____

_____

_____

_____

_____

How do you define a "right" and "wrong" decision?

"RIGHT"

....

"WRONG"

....

Where do you think you learned these definitions from?

Are these definitions helpful? If not, how would you redefine them?

What do you think it would mean about you if you made the "wrong" decision?

Which do you believe is more trustworthy: your intuition or your logic? Why? Has following the one you tend to default to been creating the experience of life you truly want?

How much do you trust yourself when making decisions?

NOT AT ALL   COMPLETELY

(1)   (2)   (3)   (4)   (5)

Why do you think that is?

_____

_____

_____

_____

_____

How often are you actually at peace with your decisions after
the fact?

NEVER   ALL OF THE TIME

(1)   (2)   (3)   (4)   (5)

Look at your answers to the previous two questions (how much
do you trust yourself / how often are you at peace). What
insights emerge from looking at these two answers together?

_____

_____

_____

_____

_____

_____

_____

Do you trust that you will be okay no matter the outcome of your choices? Why or why not?

How do you typically respond when the outcome of your decisions isn't what you hoped? How would you ideally like to respond to these situations?

Chapter 17

Understanding the Cost of Overthinking

Everything in life has a cost, but not everything is worth the price we're paying.

Which of these do you tend to prioritize most when making a decision?

- O   What will make others happy
- O   What feels safest
- O   What seems most logical
- O   What aligns with who you want to become

What parts of yourself do you abandon when you try to keep everyone else comfortable?

When trying to protect yourself from making a mistake, what characteristics emerge that you wish didn't?

What parts of yourself do you suppress or ignore when making decisions?

What do you gain by staying in indecision? What does it cost you?

GAIN	COST

What's the cost of constantly listening to fear when making decisions rather than trusting yourself?

Chapter 18

Reflection

Read through your responses and reflect on them from a lens of curiosity. What did you discover about yourself from your answers? Has the current way you've been approaching making decisions been helping or hurting you? What changes would you make? How would it feel to follow through with them?

Part 2: Self-Reinvention

Now that you've become aware of the invisible forces that have been influencing your decisions, you have the power to change them. The section you just completed revealed how you've been making decisions—often from fear, pressure, or a need to get it "right." The next section is about something deeper: choosing who you want to *be* as a decision-maker. Not a reactor to your life, but the architect of it.

Most of us have never paused to imagine what it would feel like to make decisions from peace, self-trust, and alignment. But that's exactly what this section will guide you to do. Once you clarify your values, your inner compass, and what truly expands you, you'll no longer need to search for the right answer. You'll become the kind of person who creates it.

Before you complete the next section, respond to the following question to help you begin envisioning what positive decision-making could look like:

What were some decisions you've made recently where you didn't experience overthinking in the decision-making process and simply trusted yourself? It doesn't matter if the outcome of these decisions was good or bad, what matters is how the process felt. Write them down, and they may be helpful memories to reference when answering the following questions.

Returning to Inner Knowing

*Reconnecting with the deeper guidance
that has always been within you.*

When you think about some of the best decisions that you've
made in your life, what was the process of making them like?

Think back on a time when you saw someone make a decision
that you admired. What did you admire about how they
made the decision? Was there something about their decision-
making you'd like to emulate?

What did you listen to or trust to make the decisions? Did those decisions come from logic or knowing? Safety or desire for growth?

What would it feel like to make decisions without fear, judgment, or pressure guiding the process?

How do you want to *feel* during and after making decisions, and what would you need to do to feel that way?

Chapter 20

Releasing Fears
and Old Beliefs

*Letting go of the beliefs that may have helped us
get to where we are but no longer serving us.*

What beliefs are you holding on to that make you continue
overthinking decisions?

How would your life be different if you let them go?

How would your life be different if your decisions prioritized your personal growth rather than outcomes, external success, or validation?

What would happen if you believed all external outcomes were a by-product of internal growth? How would that change how you live your life?

If no one ever praised or criticized your choices again, how would you make decisions differently?

If time didn't feel so scarce, what would you allow yourself to choose without hesitation? How would it feel to make time for this?

How can you tell when you are acting from a place of peace, alignment, and growth instead of fear? What does it feel like in your mind, body, and heart?

If your heart could speak to your mind right now, what would it say about the version of you that overthinks decisions?

Self-Trust

Rebuilding trust in your intuition, body, and truth.

How do you know when you're no longer listening to your inner truth when making a decision? What are the earliest signs?

What helps you listen to your intuition when fear is leading you in a different direction?

If fear didn't feel like a block but like a guide, where would it be trying to lead you? What is usually on the other side of fear?

What does it look like to trust yourself—not just as a feeling, but in practice?

Imagine you've made a decision and are unhappy with the outcome. What would it look like to respond to this situation from a place of nonjudgment, compassion, and flexibility instead of fear and judgment?

How would this impact your mental health and quality of life?

The Actualized Self

*To create the life you desire, choose based on
who you're becoming, not who you've been.
Rediscover your Actualized Self: the highest
potential version of yourself that chooses
from self-trust, not self-protection.*

When you imagine the most grounded, present, and aligned
version of yourself, how do they make decisions?

What questions do they ask?

What do they *not* need anymore?

If your Actualized Self were to create a set of ideal criteria to follow when making decisions, what would those be?

▷

▷

▷

▷

What are three truths your Actualized Self would want you to remember every time you face a hard decision?

1.

2.

3.

What mantras would your Actualized Self give you to help make the most aligned and expansive decisions for you?

Intention Setting

Complete the sentences:

From now on, I give myself permission to make decisions that

And I give myself permission to make decisions without *(e.g., judging or blaming myself, feeling guilty, ashamed, or unworthy)*

Chapter 24
Reflection

Read through your responses and reflect on them from a lens of curiosity. What did you discover about yourself from your answers? Has the current way you've been approaching making decisions been helping or hurting you? What changes would you make? How would it feel to give yourself permission to follow through with them?

"In any moment of decision, the best thing you can do is the right thing, the next best thing is the wrong thing, and the worst thing you can do is nothing."

—THEODORE ROOSEVELT

III.
Practicing TRUST

A Step-by-Step Exercise for When
You're Overthinking Decisions

*"The cave you fear to enter holds
the treasure you seek."*

−JOSEPH CAMPBELL

Within this section, you'll find the following:

▷ The essential *Decision-Making Principles* designed to ground you before you complete a TRUST Decision-Making Framework exercise

▷ A one-page overview of SAGE—the four dimensions of an actualized decision—to remind you to make choices that bring you the greatest peace, alignment, growth, and abundance

▷ Five repeated TRUST Decision-Making Framework exercise pages that walk you through the practice. You can continue the exercises in a separate notebook or journal, or download a printable copy.

Suggested Practice:

When you find yourself overthinking a decision and don't know what to choose, come back to this section. Begin by reading the *Decision-Making Principles* to ground yourself in truth. Then, revisit SAGE to reconnect with what matters most. Finally, complete one TRUST Decision-Making Framework exercise to gently move from confusion to clarity. The more you practice, the more familiar it will become, until trust is no longer something you search for but something you live from.

Decision-Making Principles

This is a collection of the most powerful, perspective-shifting truths in this book. These aren't just concepts to understand; they are waypoints to guide you. Lenses to see differently. Anchors to return to. Reminders of the deeper wisdom you already carry.

Read through them slowly—not just with your mind, but with your heart. Notice what resonates. What expands your perspective or gently shifts the way you think? What feels like truth?

Let each principle be more than advice. Let it be a mirror reflecting back the version of you that already knows what to do when you tune into yourself. Come back to this page whenever you feel uncertain. Not to find the "right" answer but to realign with who you are becoming. The version of you who trusts yourself. Who chooses from love, not fear. Who makes decisions not to avoid life but to fully live it.

Fear & Protection

1. The root of overthinking is fear.
2. You're not stuck in indecision because you don't know what to do. You're stuck because you're afraid of what you will lose if you choose wrong.

3. Fear is an indication not that something is wrong but that you are on the verge of something right.
4. Fear is not a stop sign—it's a compass pointing toward what matters most.
5. Fear is not in the way. It *is* the way.
6. Fear and desire are two sides of the same coin. On the other side of fear is everything you're looking for in life.
7. Fear no longer controls you the moment you decide that your peace and growth matter more than avoiding what you're afraid of.
8. Every decision is either a step into fear or a step into freedom.

Intuition & Inner Knowing

9. The mind thinks, but intuition knows.
10. The mind will convince you that you don't know what to choose even though your intuition always does.
11. The best decisions of your life will never be found in the logic of the mind. They will be felt in the intuitive knowing of your heart.
12. The clarity you seek doesn't come before making a decision. It comes *from* making a decision.
13. No one else has to understand your decision for it to be right for you.
14. Give yourself the permission you keep waiting for others to give you.

Growth, Alignment, & Choice

15. One of the greatest powers we possess is choice.
16. There are no inherently right, wrong, or perfect decisions—only ones that are aligned or unaligned.
17. At the heart of every decision is this question: Will this contract who you are, or expand who you're becoming?
18. The best decision is the one that brings the most long-term peace, alignment, and growth.
19. The purpose of life is not to get it right but to grow. The weight of the decision lifts when you realize: No matter what you choose, you're going to grow.
20. To create a life you love, make decisions based on what you want instead of making decisions to avoid what you fear.
21. No decision is final. You can always choose again.

Self-Trust & Emotional Freedom

22. If peace requires self-betrayal, it's not peace—it's people-pleasing.
23. The people who truly love you won't need you to abandon yourself to be loved by them.
24. Most advice is other people telling you what they would do—but they cannot tell you what's right for you.
25. Your focus determines your decisions.

26. Your focus is a mental magnet. What you place your attention on is what you attract more of in your life.

27. The emotion you make a decision from is the emotion you reinforce.

28. Attention is the architect of your reality.

29. No outcome is absolutely good or bad. Every outcome contains both positive and negative consequences.

30. We have power over *how* we make decisions, but not their outcomes. Who you are is determined not by what happens but by how you respond to it. Peace and confidence do not come from trying to control outcomes. They come from trusting that you will be able to navigate any outcome.

31. Ultimately, it's not the outcome that defines your path. It's your response that shapes your life.

The Dimensions of an Actualized Decision

SAGE
An actualized decision is a choice made not from fear, pressure, or the need for approval but from self-trust, presence, alignment, and love. It is the decision that brings the greatest peace and growth, not because the outcome is guaranteed, but because of who you become by choosing it.

Serenity—Which choice will give me the deepest long-term peace?
Alignment—Which choice aligns with who I want to become?
Growth—Which choice expands me the most?
Emotion—Which choice is driven by love and abundance rather than fear?

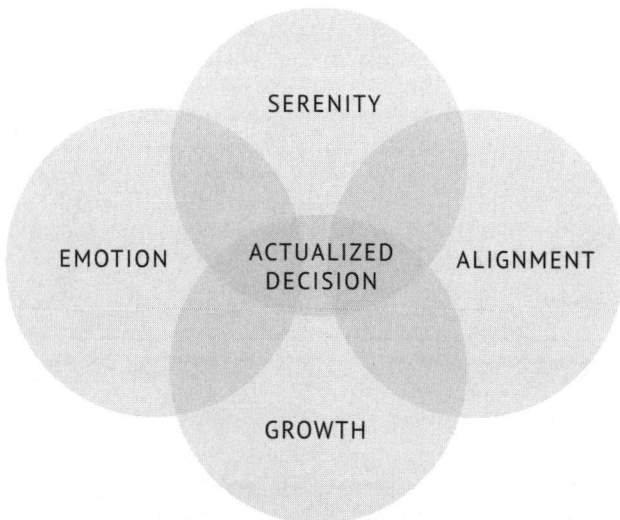

"You cannot swim for new horizons until you have courage to lose sight of the shore."

—WILLIAM FAULKNER

TRUST Decision-Making Framework

The TRUST Framework is a tool to help you make the most actualized decision—the one that brings the greatest peace, growth, and alignment. Instead of falling into the trap of chasing the "right" choice, it guides you out of overthinking and into deeper self-trust, helping you choose from intuition so that your life is shaped by your truth, not fears. Because this is an exercise you'll want to come back to on a regular basis, I recommend you write your responses in a separate notebook or journal. If you'd like a printable copy of the TRUST Decision-Making Framework, you can download one from my website at josephnguyen.org/resources

Take five deep breaths.
Regulate the nervous system by taking five slow, deep breaths. Try the two-to-one breathing technique: inhale for four seconds, and exhale for eight.

Reveal the root decision.
State the decision you are facing in one clear sentence. Don't include the possible outcomes or emotions, just the decision at hand. What event prompted this decision?

Uncover the fear and its cost.
What are you afraid might happen if you choose wrong? What do you worry that choosing wrong would mean about you?

What is this fear costing you?

Shift from fear to intuition.

Using the principles of SAGE, which choice will bring the most long-term peace, alignment, and growth—even if it feels scary to choose?

Suspend judgment and give yourself permission to consider this choice an actual possibility. How would it feel to choose this option?

If you release your attachment to outcomes and trust you can navigate whatever happens, what is your intuition telling you to choose?

Write down your actualized decision:

Take the smallest possible action.

What's the first small step you can take that will make this choice a reality?

Reflection

How did this decision feel? What did you learn about your thoughts, patterns, and fears? What did you learn about what helps you break through overthinking?

TRUST Decision-Making Framework

Take five deep breaths.
Regulate the nervous system by taking five slow, deep breaths. Try the two-to-one breathing technique: inhale for four seconds, and exhale for eight.

Reveal the root decision.
State the decision you are facing in one clear sentence. Don't include the possible outcomes or emotions, just the decision at hand. What event prompted this decision?

Uncover the fear and its cost.
What are you afraid might happen if you choose wrong? What do you worry that choosing wrong would mean about you?

What is this fear costing you?

Shift from fear to intuition.
Using the principles of SAGE, which choice will bring the most long-term peace, alignment, and growth—even if it feels scary to choose?

Suspend judgment and give yourself permission to consider this choice an actual possibility. How would it feel to choose this option?

If you release your attachment to outcomes and trust you can navigate whatever happens, what is your intuition telling you to choose?

Write down your actualized decision:

Take the smallest possible action.

What's the first small step you can take that will make this choice a reality?

Reflection

How did this decision feel? What did you learn about your thoughts, patterns, and fears? What did you learn about what helps you break through overthinking?

TRUST Decision-Making Framework

Take five deep breaths.
Regulate the nervous system by taking five slow, deep breaths. Try the two-to-one breathing technique: inhale for four seconds, and exhale for eight.

Reveal the root decision.
State the decision you are facing in one clear sentence. Don't include the possible outcomes or emotions, just the decision at hand. What event prompted this decision?

Uncover the fear and its cost.
What are you afraid might happen if you choose wrong? What do you worry that choosing wrong would mean about you?

What is this fear costing you?

Shift from fear to intuition.
Using the principles of SAGE, which choice will bring the most long-term peace, alignment, and growth—even if it feels scary to choose?

Suspend judgment and give yourself permission to consider this choice an actual possibility. How would it feel to choose this option?

If you release your attachment to outcomes and trust you can navigate whatever happens, what is your intuition telling you to choose?

Write down your actualized decision:

Take the smallest possible action.
What's the first small step you can take that will make this choice a reality?

Reflection
How did this decision feel? What did you learn about your thoughts, patterns, and fears? What did you learn about what helps you break through overthinking?

TRUST Decision-Making Framework

Take five deep breaths.
Regulate the nervous system by taking five slow, deep breaths. Try the two-to-one breathing technique: inhale for four seconds, and exhale for eight.

Reveal the root decision.
State the decision you are facing in one clear sentence. Don't include the possible outcomes or emotions, just the decision at hand. What event prompted this decision?

Uncover the fear and its cost.
What are you afraid might happen if you choose wrong? What do you worry that choosing wrong would mean about you?

What is this fear costing you?

Shift from fear to intuition.
Using the principles of SAGE, which choice will bring the most long-term peace, alignment, and growth—even if it feels scary to choose?

Suspend judgment and give yourself permission to consider this choice an actual possibility. How would it feel to choose this option?

If you release your attachment to outcomes and trust you can navigate whatever happens, what is your intuition telling you to choose?

Write down your actualized decision:

Take the smallest possible action.
What's the first small step you can take that will make this choice a reality?

Reflection
How did this decision feel? What did you learn about your thoughts, patterns, and fears? What did you learn about what helps you break through overthinking?

TRUST Decision-Making Framework

Take five deep breaths.
Regulate the nervous system by taking five slow, deep breaths. Try the two-to-one breathing technique: inhale for four seconds, and exhale for eight.

Reveal the root decision.
State the decision you are facing in one clear sentence. Don't include the possible outcomes or emotions, just the decision at hand. What event prompted this decision?

Uncover the fear and its cost.
What are you afraid might happen if you choose wrong? What do you worry that choosing wrong would mean about you?

What is this fear costing you?

Shift from fear to intuition.
Using the principles of SAGE, which choice will bring the most long-term peace, alignment, and growth—even if it feels scary to choose?

Suspend judgment and give yourself permission to consider this choice an actual possibility. How would it feel to choose this option?

If you release your attachment to outcomes and trust you can navigate whatever happens, what is your intuition telling you to choose?

Write down your actualized decision:

Take the smallest possible action.
What's the first small step you can take that will make this choice a reality?

Reflection
How did this decision feel? What did you learn about your thoughts, patterns, and fears? What did you learn about what helps you break through overthinking?

Reflection

Take a moment and go through the last five exercises you filled out and notice the patterns, shifts, and insights that have emerged. This is your chance to pause and witness what's changing and growing—not just in your decisions, but in you. Let this be a space to become mindful of what's working, what's ready to be released, and what's asking for more of your trust.

Progress Check-In

How much was overthinking present in these decisions?

CONSTANTLY   NOT AT ALL

(1)   (2)   (3)   (4)   (5)

How much did you trust yourself in these decisions compared to before this process?

MUCH LESS   MUCH MORE

(1)   (2)   (3)   (4)   (5)

How much were you able to trust that you'd be able to handle the outcomes of the decisions, even if they weren't the ones you desired?

MUCH LESS   COMPLETELY

(1)   (2)   (3)   (4)   (5)

How different does your decision-making feel now compared to before this process?

NO CHANGE   COMPLETELY TRANSFORMED

(1)   (2)   (3)   (4)   (5)

Self-Reflection

Which decision felt the hardest? Did you recognize any patterns in your thoughts or fears in those moments? What insights can you draw from these experiences?

What makes overthinking worse when making decisions? What helps you let go of overthinking decisions and trust yourself? How can you bring more of that into future decisions?

What did it feel like in the moments when you followed your intuition rather than fear? What did you learn from those experiences?

If this page marked the end of one old belief, story, or way of being, what would it be? What are you ready to leave behind?

How have you felt your decision-making change over the course of working through these exercises?

What do you want to remember the next time you're facing a challenging decision that would help you most?

"You may not control all the events that happen to you, but you can decide not to be reduced by them."

—MAYA ANGELOU

IV.
Tiny Acts of Self-Trust

Mini-Decision-Making Experiments to Help You Stop Overthinking and Start Trusting Yourself Again

"The greatest mistake you can make in life is to be continually fearing that you will make one."

—ELBERT HUBBARD

This section contains a series of insightful miniexperiments designed to be both playful and profound—inviting you into everyday scenarios where you can safely practice trusting yourself and your intuition.

While knowledge comes through understanding, wisdom is born through experience. These challenges help translate what you've learned in the book into embodied insight, turning ideas into inner shifts and reflections into new ways of being. What may seem like a small act on the surface often becomes a powerful catalyst beneath it. You might be surprised by how these subtle choices begin to reshape how you see yourself, how you make decisions, and how deeply you're capable of living in alignment with who you truly are.

"The privilege of a lifetime is to become who you truly are."

—CARL JUNG

Flip a Coin and
Follow the Feeling

Think of a decision you're currently facing. Assign heads and tails to the two options, then flip the coin. But before you look at the result, pause. Ask yourself: *What do I hope it lands on?* Just noticing your answer can be revealing.

Now look at the coin and see the result. How do you feel about the option that was chosen for you? Are you relieved? Disappointed? Surprised? Your reaction reveals the answer you subconsciously wanted before your mind had a chance to overanalyze or second-guess.

This experiment isn't about leaving your choice to chance. It's about learning to trust the truth already within you.

Planning

Use this space to plan out how you will complete this exercise. What decision will you use it for? If your mind tries to talk you out of it, what truth can you remind yourself of in that moment to stay committed to this experiment?

Reflection

Use this space to reflect on how the experiment went. How did it go? What surprised you? How did it feel to complete it? What did you learn about yourself through the experience? What insights do you want to take from this that would be most helpful for future decisions?

Go with Your Gut for Food

The next time you're at a restaurant (or deciding what to eat), choose the first thing that genuinely speaks to you before scanning every option, comparing, or calculating what's "best." Let yourself order without overthinking, without needing it to be perfect.

This exercise is a practice of trusting your gut—literally. Notice how it feels to honor your first instinct instead of trying to overanalyze the choice. Even something as simple as choosing a meal can be a doorway to more ease, more self-trust, and more presence with what's in front of you.

Planning

Use this space to plan out how you will complete this exercise. When will you do it? If your mind tries to talk you out of it, what truth can you remind yourself of in that moment to stay committed to this experiment?

Reflection

Use this space to reflect on how the experiment went. How did it go? What surprised you? How did it feel to complete it? What did you learn about yourself through the experience? What insights do you want to take from this that would be most helpful for future decisions?

Follow a Tiny Spark

Say yes to something small that sparks your curiosity or excitement—something that feels oddly compelling, even if it doesn't make logical sense. Maybe it's a book you feel pulled toward, a side street you've never explored, or an idea that lights you up for no obvious reason.

This experiment isn't about being practical, it's about honoring energy over logic and learning to listen to what you *want* to do instead of what you think you *should* do. When you follow those quiet, expansive sparks, you create space for joy, surprise, and growth. Over time, this practice teaches you that what feels alive is often far more worthwhile than what merely makes sense.

Planning

Use this space to plan out how you will complete this exercise. When will you do it? If your mind tries to talk you out of it, what truth can you remind yourself of in that moment to stay committed to this experiment?

Reflection

Use this space to reflect on how the experiment went. How did it go? What surprised you? How did it feel to complete it? What did you learn about yourself through the experience? What insights do you want to take from this that would be most helpful for future decisions?

"The risk of a wrong decision is preferable to the terror of indecision."

—MAIMONIDES

Choose Without Research

For one small decision today—what to buy, where to eat, which option to pick—resist the urge to read reviews, check ratings, or ask for anyone else's opinion. Just pause, tune in, and choose what feels right in the moment without gathering more data. Then observe *how* you feel, both before and after the choice. Notice whether peace, tension, or clarity arises, not from what you chose, but from how you chose it. This is a gentle way to practice trusting your internal compass before outsourcing your knowing to the outside world.

Planning

Use this space to plan out how you will complete this exercise. When will you do it? If your mind tries to talk you out of it, what truth can you remind yourself of in that moment to stay committed to this experiment?

Reflection

Use this space to reflect on how the experiment went. How did it go? What surprised you? How did it feel to complete it? What did you learn about yourself through the experience? What insights do you want to take from this that would be most helpful for future decisions?

Walk Without a Destination

Set aside 15 minutes to take a walk with no phone, no plan, and no destination. Don't map the route or decide in advance where you'll go. Just step outside and see where your feet take you. Follow whatever path calls to you, even if it doesn't "make sense." Let the walk be aimless, curious, and unhurried. Look at things as if you are seeing them through the eyes of a child for the first time.

During the walk, practice presence. Gently release any thoughts about what you need to do next. You don't have to solve anything or be productive right now. This is a practice of letting life unfold without needing to control it. Often, the moments that we remember most aren't the ones we planned but the ones where we were the most present. When life stops being a means to an end and becomes a joy in itself, peace finds its way back in. Notice how you feel during and after. What shifts when you no longer have anywhere to be but here?

Planning

Use this space to plan out how you will complete this exercise. When will you do it? If your mind tries to talk you out of it, what truth can you remind yourself of in that moment to stay committed to this experiment?

Reflection

Use this space to reflect on how the experiment went. How did it go? What surprised you? How did it feel to complete it? What did you learn about yourself through the experience? What insights do you want to take from this that would be most helpful for future decisions?

Ask for What You Need

Choose one small need you usually ignore or suppress and express it to someone else. It could be as simple as, "Can we pause for a minute?" "I need a little space," "Can we reschedule?" or "I'd actually prefer this instead."

It doesn't have to be dramatic. It just has to be honest. Each time you voice a need—especially in the small moments—you affirm to yourself that your well-being matters and that you can make choices that honor it. Self-trust deepens when you stop abandoning yourself in the name of staying connected and start building connections that include you, too.

Planning

Use this space to plan out how you will complete this exercise. When will you do it? If your mind tries to talk you out of it, what truth can you remind yourself of in that moment to stay committed to this experiment?

Reflection

Use this space to reflect on how the experiment went. How did it go? What surprised you? How did it feel to complete it? What did you learn about yourself through the experience? What insights do you want to take from this that would be most helpful for future decisions?

Write Without Editing

Set a timer for five minutes and free-write on a piece of paper about a decision or feeling you've been struggling with. As you write, don't erase, don't censor. Let the words come exactly as they are: messy, tangled, unsure. Often, the truth spills out when we stop trying to say it perfectly.

Once it's all on the page, take a breath and read what you wrote. There's often a surprising sense of relief that comes when the noise in your head becomes something you can see with your eyes. What stands out to you? What patterns or insights emerge? And most importantly, what is your intuition whispering beneath the overthinking?

Planning

Use this space to plan out how you will complete this exercise. When will you do it? If your mind tries to talk you out of it, what truth can you remind yourself of in that moment to stay committed to this experiment?

Reflection

Use this space to reflect on how the experiment went. How did it go? What surprised you? How did it feel to complete it? What did you learn about yourself through the experience? What insights do you want to take from this that would be most helpful for future decisions?

"*There is freedom waiting for you, on the breezes of the sky. And you ask 'What if I fall?' Oh but my darling, what if you fly?*"

—ERIN HANSON

Follow Your Inner Child

When we were young, we followed what felt fun, exciting, or curious without needing a reason why. We played, explored, created, and changed our minds freely. But somewhere along the way, many of us traded that joy for practicality and logic. We began suppressing the parts of ourselves that once made us feel alive. And then we wondered why everything started to feel so serious and heavy.

This experiment is simple: give yourself permission to do one thing today that your inner child would love. Something that may not be "productive" or make sense to anyone else. Maybe it's returning to a hobby you once loved, rewatching a movie you remember fondly, dancing around your living room to a favorite song from when you were growing up, or pulling out old photos, drawings, or letters and letting yourself remember who you were before the world told you who to be.

It doesn't need to take your whole day. But offering even a moment to this part of you—without judgment or justification—can nourish your spirit in ways logic never will. What would make your inner child smile today? Let yourself have that. Then notice how it feels to come alive again.

Planning

Use this space to plan out how you will complete this exercise. When will you do it? If your mind tries to talk you out of it, what truth can you remind yourself of in that moment to stay committed to this experiment?

Reflection

Use this space to reflect on how the experiment went. How did it go? What surprised you? How did it feel to complete it? What did you learn about yourself through the experience? What insights do you want to take from this that would be most helpful for future decisions?

Ask Yourself Instead of Someone Else

The next time you feel the urge to ask for someone else's opinion, pause. Before reaching out, turn inward and ask: Do I really need an outside perspective? What do I already know? What would I choose if I fully trusted myself?

This isn't about always having the right answer, it's about practicing the art of being your own source. Every time you check in with yourself first, you strengthen the quiet muscle of self-trust. Over time, it becomes easier to hear your voice— even when the world is loud.

Planning

Use this space to plan out how you will complete this exercise. When will you do it? If your mind tries to talk you out of it, what truth can you remind yourself of in that moment to stay committed to this experiment?

Reflection

Use this space to reflect on how the experiment went. How did it go? What surprised you? How did it feel to complete it? What did you learn about yourself through the experience? What insights do you want to take from this that would be most helpful for future decisions?

The Courage to Say No

Say a gentle no to something small today—something you'd normally say yes to out of guilt or habit. Maybe it's continuing a text conversation you don't have energy for or agreeing to a minor favor you don't want to do. This time, don't overexplain or justify. Simply say, *"I'm not able to right now,"* and let that be enough. Then, give yourself full permission to not feel guilty—for protecting your energy, for honoring your peace, for listening to yourself.

Afterward, pause and reflect. How did you feel right before saying no? And how did you feel after? What shifted when you allowed yourself to release the guilt?

Planning

Use this space to plan out how you will complete this exercise. When will you do it? If your mind tries to talk you out of it, what truth can you remind yourself of in that moment to stay committed to this experiment?

Reflection

Use this space to reflect on how the experiment went. How did it go? What surprised you? How did it feel to complete it? What did you learn about yourself through the experience? What insights do you want to take from this that would be most helpful for future decisions?

Choose Presence over Productivity

Set aside one hour today to be completely unproductive—on purpose. No multitasking, no crossing things off a list, no optimizing. Just sit, breathe, sip tea, lie on the floor, stare out the window, go for a walk, visit a park, and. Let yourself be.

This isn't about abandoning your responsibilities. It's about remembering that your worth isn't tied to how much you accomplish. Giving yourself even one hour of true rest can restore the energy, clarity, and presence you bring to everything else. Let this be your quiet reminder that everything will still get done, but from a place that feels less stressful and more grounded.

Planning

Use this space to plan out how you will complete this exercise. When will you do it? If your mind tries to talk you out of it, what truth can you remind yourself of in that moment to stay committed to this experiment?

Reflection

Use this space to reflect on how the experiment went. How did it go? What surprised you? How did it feel to complete it? What did you learn about yourself through the experience? What insights do you want to take from this that would be most helpful for future decisions?

Voice a Preference Out Loud

The next time someone asks what you'd like—where to sit, what to eat, what to do—voice your preference instead of defaulting to what others want. Don't overthink it. Don't minimize it. Just say what you'd genuinely prefer, even if it's as simple as, *"I'd rather sit over here,"* or *"I'd love to do this instead."*

Most of the time, it's not an inconvenience, it's just a choice. And giving yourself permission to choose without guilt is a powerful act of self-trust. Every time you allow yourself to take up space, you reinforce this truth: your needs matter just as much as anyone else's.

Planning

Use this space to plan out how you will complete this exercise. When will you do it? If your mind tries to talk you out of it, what truth can you remind yourself of in that moment to stay committed to this experiment?

Reflection

Use this space to reflect on how the experiment went. How did it go? What surprised you? How did it feel to complete it? What did you learn about yourself through the experience? What insights do you want to take from this that would be most helpful for future decisions?

Follow Through on a Promise to Yourself

Choose one small but meaningful thing you've been wanting to do—move your body, rest without guilt, make time for a creative hobby—and write it down as a promise to yourself: "Today, I will…"

Then do it. Not because you have to, but because you said you would. It doesn't matter how big or small the action is. What matters is that you honored your word to yourself.

Self-trust isn't built through achievement; it's built through showing up for yourself again and again in quiet, consistent ways. This is how you become someone you can count on.

Planning

Use this space to plan out how you will complete this exercise. When will you do it? If your mind tries to talk you out of it, what truth can you remind yourself of in that moment to stay committed to this experiment?

Reflection

Use this space to reflect on how the experiment went. How did it go? What surprised you? How did it feel to complete it? What did you learn about yourself through the experience? What insights do you want to take from this that would be most helpful for future decisions?

"You don't have to see the whole staircase, just take the first step."

—MARTIN LUTHER KING JR.

Break One Tiny Habit
(on Purpose)

What's one small habit you've been repeating that no longer feels aligned with who you want to be? Something that drains you, distracts you, or keeps you stuck on autopilot? Today, interrupt that pattern just once. Step outside instead of reaching for your phone. Pause before responding how you usually would. Allow yourself to simply be bored and rest for a bit without needing to distract yourself. Do the opposite of what the old pattern expects.

You don't have to overhaul your life, just create a single microdisruption. Notice how it feels to *choose* rather than operate by default. Even the smallest break in routine can remind you: you are the one steering this life. You can shift, even slightly, toward more peace, more presence, more intention.

Planning

Use this space to plan out how you will complete this exercise. When will you do it? If your mind tries to talk you out of it, what truth can you remind yourself of in that moment to stay committed to this experiment?

Reflection

Use this space to reflect on how the experiment went. How did it go? What surprised you? How did it feel to complete it? What did you learn about yourself through the experience? What insights do you want to take from this that would be most helpful for future decisions?

Set an 80% Rule

Today, choose one decision to make when you feel only 80% sure of your choice and let that be enough. Don't chase the final 20% of certainty. You don't need all the information to move forward. You only need enough.

Waiting for absolute clarity often leads to inaction, not better choices. This experiment invites you to act with what you know now and trust yourself to adjust as you go. Progress comes not from perfection, but from choosing and learning in motion.

Planning

Use this space to plan out how you will complete this exercise. When will you do it? If your mind tries to talk you out of it, what truth can you remind yourself of in that moment to stay committed to this experiment?

Reflection

Use this space to reflect on how the experiment went. How did it go? What surprised you? How did it feel to complete it? What did you learn about yourself through the experience? What insights do you want to take from this that would be most helpful for future decisions?

Delay the Decision on Purpose

Choose a decision you feel pressure to make and deliberately delay it for 24 hours. Not to procrastinate or ruminate, but to pause, on purpose. Give yourself full permission not to think about it until tomorrow. No spiraling, no problem-solving. Just space.

When the next day arrives, return to the decision with fresh eyes. What's different now? Has anything shifted? Your clarity, your emotional state, the decision itself? Notice what changes when you trust time to clarify instead of scrambling to fix. Sometimes the pressure lifts simply because you allowed it to.

Planning

Use this space to plan out how you will complete this exercise. When will you do it? If your mind tries to talk you out of it, what truth can you remind yourself of in that moment to stay committed to this experiment?

Reflection

Use this space to reflect on how the experiment went. How did it go? What surprised you? How did it feel to complete it? What did you learn about yourself through the experience? What insights do you want to take from this that would be most helpful for future decisions?

"Once you make a decision, the universe conspires to make it happen."

—RALPH WALDO EMERSON

Take Aligned Action
Before You Feel "Ready"

Choose one small action that moves you closer to something you care about. Send the message. Open the document. Make the call. Whatever it is, do it before you feel fully certain or ready.

Most of us wait for clarity like it's a permission slip. But clarity is often what follows the choice, not what precedes it. The more you try to think your way into certainty, the further away it drifts. Action reveals what overthinking hides. You learn faster by doing. You adjust more easily in motion. And some doors only appear once you're already walking.

Planning

Use this space to plan out how you will complete this exercise. When will you do it? If your mind tries to talk you out of it, what truth can you remind yourself of in that moment to stay committed to this experiment?

Reflection

Use this space to reflect on how the experiment went. How did it go? What surprised you? How did it feel to complete it? What did you learn about yourself through the experience? What insights do you want to take from this that would be most helpful for future decisions?

Do One Thing for Yourself

Do one thing for yourself just because you want to. Not because it's productive. Not because it makes sense. Not because someone else asked or approved. But simply because you want to.

Today, give yourself permission to do something you've been longing to do—something small or big that you've talked yourself out of, convinced yourself was silly, indulgent, or unnecessary. Maybe it felt like a waste of time or money. But if it brings even a flicker of joy, that's more than enough of a reason.

When you stop suppressing the part of you that craves play, adventure, beauty, or rest, you learn to listen to your desires again. You begin making space for aliveness—for joy, for wonder, for the kind of moments that don't need to be useful to be meaningful.

Let today be a gift to yourself, for no other reason than because your desire matters.

Planning

Use this space to plan out how you will complete this exercise. When will you do it? If your mind tries to talk you out of it, what truth can you remind yourself of in that moment to stay committed to this experiment?

Reflection

Use this space to reflect on how the experiment went. How did it go? What surprised you? How did it feel to complete it? What did you learn about yourself through the experience? What insights do you want to take from this that would be most helpful for future decisions?

Ask a Question You're Scared to Know the Answer To

Bring to mind a question you've been avoiding—something you've been too afraid to ask out loud, whether in conversation, in your journal, or quietly within your own heart. Let this moment be your permission to finally ask it.

We often avoid these questions because we fear the answer might hurt, catalyze change, or reveal a truth we're not ready to face. But most of the time, the fear of the answer is louder than the answer itself. And when we finally face it, we realize that we can handle more than we thought.

You don't need to force clarity or action right away. Just begin by asking and holding space for whatever comes up. This is how we build self-trust—not by controlling the answers, but by being willing to hear them and knowing we can handle whatever they may be.

Planning

Use this space to plan out how you will complete this exercise. When will you do it? If your mind tries to talk you out of it, what truth can you remind yourself of in that moment to stay committed to this experiment?

Reflection

Use this space to reflect on how the experiment went. How did it go? What surprised you? How did it feel to complete it? What did you learn about yourself through the experience? What insights do you want to take from this that would be most helpful for future decisions?

A Day of Trusting Your Intuition

For one full day, make a conscious commitment: whenever a decision comes up—big or small—choose to follow your intuition rather than overanalyzing. Don't spiral into pros and cons. Don't wait for certainty. Just feel for what resonates, and go with it. Of course, stay safe and grounded; this isn't about being reckless. But most choices we face aren't life-threatening; they're invitations to build trust with ourselves. As the day unfolds, pay close attention to how you feel both during and after each decision. Does acting on intuition bring a sense of freedom or unease? Does it spark relief, joy, or clarity? How does it feel to go a day living your life intuitively rather than analytically?

Planning

Use this space to plan out how you will complete this exercise. When will you do it? If your mind tries to talk you out of it, what truth can you remind yourself of in that moment to stay committed to this experiment?

Reflection

Use this space to reflect on how the experiment went. How did it go? What surprised you? How did it feel to complete it? What did you learn about yourself through the experience? What insights do you want to take from this that would be most helpful for future decisions?

Create Your Own Mini-Experiment

Design a small experiment that might help you overthink your decisions a little less. It could be something out of your usual routine—a tiny stretch beyond your comfort zone—or a bigger leap you've quietly wanted to take but haven't given yourself permission to try.

Let it be something that doesn't need to make sense to anyone else. Maybe it has no obvious purpose. Maybe it doesn't feel "productive." But if it brings even a little peace, play, or freedom to your day, that's more than enough.

This is your space to choose. What's one thing you'd love to try, just for you?

Planning

Use this space to plan out how you will complete this exercise. When will you do it? If your mind tries to talk you out of it, what truth can you remind yourself of in that moment to stay committed to this experiment?

Reflection

Use this space to reflect on how the experiment went. How did it go? What surprised you? How did it feel to complete it? What did you learn about yourself through the experience? What insights do you want to take from this that would be most helpful for future decisions?

Create Your Own Mini-Experiment

Design a small experiment that might help you overthink your decisions a little less. It could be something out of your usual routine—a tiny stretch beyond your comfort zone—or a bigger leap you've quietly wanted to take but haven't given yourself permission to try.

Let it be something that doesn't need to make sense to anyone else. Maybe it has no obvious purpose. Maybe it doesn't feel "productive." But if it brings even a little peace, play, or freedom to your day, that's more than enough.

This is your space to choose. What's one thing you'd love to try, just for you?

Planning

Use this space to plan out how you will complete this exercise. When will you do it? If your mind tries to talk you out of it, what truth can you remind yourself of in that moment to stay committed to this experiment?

Reflection

Use this space to reflect on how the experiment went. How did it go? What surprised you? How did it feel to complete it? What did you learn about yourself through the experience? What insights do you want to take from this that would be most helpful for future decisions?

Create Your Own Mini-Experiment

Design a small experiment that might help you overthink your decisions a little less. It could be something out of your usual routine—a tiny stretch beyond your comfort zone—or a bigger leap you've quietly wanted to take but haven't given yourself permission to try.

Let it be something that doesn't need to make sense to anyone else. Maybe it has no obvious purpose. Maybe it doesn't feel "productive." But if it brings even a little peace, play, or freedom to your day, that's more than enough.

This is your space to choose. What's one thing you'd love to try, just for you?

Planning

Use this space to plan out how you will complete this exercise. When will you do it? If your mind tries to talk you out of it, what truth can you remind yourself of in that moment to stay committed to this experiment?

Reflection

Use this space to reflect on how the experiment went. How did it go? What surprised you? How did it feel to complete it? What did you learn about yourself through the experience? What insights do you want to take from this that would be most helpful for future decisions?

What Should You Read Next?

Thank you from the bottom of my heart for taking the time to read this book. If you enjoyed it, I highly recommend checking out my first book, *Don't Believe Everything You Think (Expanded Edition)*, which explores how to break free from anxiety and self-doubt.

Every week, I share a new piece of writing through my "Nuggets of Wisdom" newsletter, which contains one simple, perspective-shifting idea to expand your mind and help you find more peace, joy, and abundance.

Subscribers are also the first to hear about my newest books and projects.

Join our community of seekers and sign up for my newsletter at josephnguyen.org/newsletter.

Or you may sign up by scanning the QR code below:

Don't Believe
Everything
You Think

BOOKS BY JOSEPH NGUYEN:

*Don't Believe Everything You Think: Why Your
Thinking Is the Beginning & End of Suffering*

*Beyond Thoughts: An Exploration of
Who We Are beyond Our Minds*

*Healing Anxiety & Overthinking Journal & Workbook:
Let Go of Anxiety, Overcome Fear,
Find Peace & End Suffering*

*Boundaries = Freedom: How to Create Boundaries
That Set You Free without Feeling Guilty*

*The Art of Creating: How to Create Art That
Transforms Yourself and the World*

**You may find my books, courses, and newsletter
on my website: josephnguyen.org**

Don't Believe Everything You Think

Why Your Thinking Is the Beginning & End of Suffering

Expanded Edition

Joseph Nguyen

AUTHORS EQUITY

For Kenna,
who taught me what unconditional love
truly is and how it can change the world

Contents

Preface to the Expanded Edition

I wrote *Don't Believe Everything You Think* to save myself from my own mind. For as long as I could remember, I never knew what life was like without chronic fear and anxiety. No matter how I tried to change my thinking, I always felt the same—anxious, frustrated, and stressed. It wasn't until I stopped fighting my mind and began trying to *understand* it that things began to change. What I discovered transformed my relationship with my mind forever. What had been my worst enemy became my best friend.

My intention when I released the first edition of this book was to share what I had found and hopefully help others experience freedom from their anxious minds. To me, if the book helped even one person, it would have been a success.

I never expected that in just two years, the book would reach over seven hundred thousand people across the world in dozens of different countries and be translated into over forty languages. Every day, I am overwhelmed with gratitude for how much love the book has received and how often readers have shared it with their friends and family. I cannot thank each reader enough for their kindness and generosity.

As the book continued to spread, I received thousands of messages of gratitude from readers and countless questions. I did my best to respond to as many of them as possible, and many of those I replied to noted how helpful my responses were. And so when the opportunity arose, I decided to revise and expand the book to address all of these thoughtful questions readers had. The result, I hope, is a book that helps readers more profoundly on their journey to find peace.

In this expanded edition, I added more examples, thought experiments, frameworks, and deeper explanations of many topics readers wanted to know more about. Poems throughout now provide another dimension for reflection on the book's ideas.

One of the questions I received most frequently was about how to practically apply these concepts in daily life, so I've added a whole chapter that walks readers step-by-step through a methodology to help them let go of negative thinking in the simplest way possible. The book now also includes a final section of practical exercises designed to help readers practice and integrate the book's teachings into their lives more easily and seamlessly.

I sincerely hope this book helps you as much as it has helped me. Thank you for allowing me to be on this journey with you, and I cannot wait to meet you within the pages.

With All My Love,

Joseph

most of us only change
when the pain of holding on to what we're
    attached to is greater than the fear of the
        unknown

Introduction

What You Will Discover in This Book

We cannot change what we are not aware of, and once we are aware, we cannot help but change.

—SHERYL SANDBERG

You know the feeling.

You sit down to accomplish a simple work task, and suddenly, you are flooded with thoughts of doubt and self-criticism. Why didn't you do this task earlier? You're not good enough—you're probably going to fail at this task anyway. What if people find out that you don't really know what you're doing? Why did they get a promotion and you didn't?

At a company meeting you try to be present, but you're consumed with thoughts of how much you hate your job. You want to quit and follow that dream you've always had, but you know there's no way you could succeed in that. It'll never happen, and besides, giving up your job is too risky. You'd rather suffer in certainty than live with the fear of uncertainty. It's better to not try at all than to try and fail, right?

But it's not just about work. As you go about your day, this thinking follows you. An interaction with a friend causes you to spiral. Why did you say that? Why are they even friends with you? Do they think you're weird? Did you say the wrong thing? Are they talking behind your back? Why are you so different from them? Why is it so hard to find friends? What if you end up alone?

As you get home, you scroll on your mobile device and see dozens of picture-perfect posts—all of which are reminding you of everything you don't have, how the world is getting worse, and how everyone else's lives seem to be better than yours. Why do you feel so behind? Why does it seem like everyone has their life together and you don't? When will things start working out for you?

By the time you reach the end of your day, you're exhausted. Your mind has been in overdrive all day, overthinking, overanalyzing, judging every decision you make. Now, lying in bed, the rumination continues, and you can't sleep. All you want is a moment of peace. To be able to let go of the anxiety and over-thinking that consume your days. The vicious cycles of doubt, shame, and anger. To be able to feel the joy, fulfillment, and peace that always seem just out of reach.

But that kind of change feels impossible. You've been trying your whole life, but nothing has lessened the mental suffering you experience every day. You've concluded that life is suffering, and that's all there is to it.

Everything feels hopeless.

But this is only half the story. The narrative you are living can be changed at any time because it is being written in real time—by you.

Life does not have to be this way. Life is not suffering. Suffering is *part* of life, but it does not have to be the majority of it.

You are not fundamentally broken. You are not a problem to be fixed but a human who is meant to be understood. Through understanding yourself and how your experience of life is created in the mind, you can find peace.

How do I know this? Because it has been my journey as well. I refused to believe that this was all life was, so I dedicated mine to discovering how to end my own psychological and emotional suffering. On that path, I found more questions than answers.

What is suffering? Why do we suffer? What is the root cause of suffering? Is there an "off" button for this kind of rumination in the brain? How can we stop overthinking? Can anyone find peace, or is it only reserved for those who believe in certain religions, become monks, or attain enlightenment? Is it possible to find peace no matter what happens to us in life?

These are the core questions that drove me to write this book—to save myself and hopefully help others do the same.

This book was written to help you find those answers for yourself and finally find the peace you've been searching for.

This is a bold statement, I know, but I have complete confidence that you will not be the same person after reading this book. The only constant in life is change; growth is inevitable. And so no matter who you are, where you're from, what you have or haven't done, what you have or don't have, I know from the depths of my soul that you can find peace, unconditional love, fulfillment, and an abundance of joy in life.

I promise that this includes you, even if it doesn't feel that way yet. Love knows no boundaries. An open mind and a willing heart are all you need to receive every answer you've been seeking. There are, of course, practical benefits to reducing the mental suffering in our lives: succeeding in our careers or work, building deeper and more harmonious relationships, overcoming lifelong addictions, letting go of destructive habits, and increasing our health, vitality, and overall energy.

Yet these external results are not the point of this book. They are byproducts of understanding how our minds work and reducing the mental turmoil that stops us from creating a life we love.

And more importantly, if we dig deeper, we see that most of our yearnings for approval, money, and significance stem from a desire to experience certain feelings. Feelings such as love, joy, peace, freedom, and fulfillment.

These feelings are what we truly want; the psychological trap lies in believing that only external things will give us those feelings. The key is focusing on the feelings themselves and realizing how our emotions can be independent of our environment.

Don't read this book for information; read it for insight. Insight (wisdom) can only be found within. That is why it is called *in*sight (*in*side). I will not tell you anything you don't already know deep inside your soul. To find everything you're looking for in life, you must look inside yourself and discover the wisdom that already exists within you. That is where the truth is found. This book is merely a guide to help you know where to look.

The journey begins with the hope that a better life is possible. Without hope, we have nothing, so the fact that you're here, reading this now, is a testament to your faith, courage, and strength. I know with absolute certainty that you will find what you're looking for if you continue on your path with the belief you have in your heart.

The words in this book are not the truth; they point to the truth. Truth cannot be intellectualized; it can only be experienced. It is within everyone and everything. But you must look beyond the form (the physical) to see and experience the truth (the spiritual).

Look beyond the words. Truth comes in the form of a feeling. **Look for that feeling.** From that feeling will come the wisdom you seek, which will set you free. And that's what we're all ultimately seeking, isn't it?

Many who discover the truth describe the feeling as a resonance in your heart and a sense of alignment and harmony with who you truly are. It is an experience of peace and liberation. They say it's the most familiar unfamiliar feeling, like you're finally home. It is the feeling of discovering that which you already know.

This book may seem simple. In fact, the solutions I propose may seem almost too simple, and your mind (ego) may try to fight them or attempt to make them complex. When that time comes, I want you to remember that the truth is always simple.

If you want to find the truth, look for simplicity. Approach this book with an open mind and a heart of pure intention to know the truth, and you'll receive everything you've been searching for.

This book is designed to help you discover the root cause of your mental suffering—and how we all have the power to choose a new experience. To solve a problem, you first need to understand it deeply, and so, for this reason, much of this book is spent describing this insight.

But I also want to give you tools that will make it easier to apply these ideas in your life and create the transformation you seek. That is where the "Practice" section at the end of this book comes into play. It is your toolbox, with guides, prompts, and exercises that offer tangible, step-by-step help to allow you to find more peace, love, and joy in your life. As you make them a part of your daily practice, the change you desire will become inevitable.

Before we move on, I want to express my deepest gratitude to you for being here and sharing your time and attention with me. Those are some of the most valuable gifts you could give to another. Thank you for that gift to me, which you are also giving to yourself. Never forget your own divinity, because it is only through our divinity that we have our humanity.

From My Heart to Yours,

Joseph

Chapter 1

The Journey to Discovering the Root Cause of Suffering

*People have a hard time letting go of their
suffering. Out of a fear of the unknown,
they prefer suffering that is familiar.*

—THICH NHAT HANH

Before we can explore how to end our suffering, we first have to understand what we mean by suffering. *Suffering* is not the same as *pain*, and understanding the distinction between the two is the key to realizing that no matter what happens in life, we do not have to suffer emotionally and psychologically. A Buddhist teaching helps explain this concept.

It is said that two arrows fly our way whenever we experience a negative event. Being struck by the first arrow hurts—that arrow is pain. The second arrow is our emotional reaction to the first, and often, it is even more painful than the first arrow. That second arrow is where suffering originates from.

The Buddha explained, "In life, we can't always control the first arrow. However, the second arrow is our reaction to the first. The second arrow is optional."

In other words, pain is unavoidable, but how we react to that pain is up to us, and that reaction will dictate whether or not we suffer. Now, I'm not saying that the difficult experiences we've been through are all in our heads. On the contrary, terrible and unfortunate things happen to people every single day. I'm saying that although we inevitably experience pain in our lives, *suffering* is optional. And it is this suffering from which we can learn to free ourselves.

When I first heard the story of the two arrows, it was a revelation. It gave me a new way to understand the suffering I was experiencing. The problem wasn't the pain itself; it was in my *reaction* to the pain.

But this excitement was quickly followed by a new wave of confusion. How could I simply choose not to suffer? If it were as easy as that, no one would suffer anymore.

On my journey to find peace, I came across many teachings, studies, and methods that promised to eliminate this suffering. I read dozens, if not hundreds, of books; studied psychology and philosophy; talked to therapists; and tried changing my habits—waking up at 4 a.m., following a vegan diet, becoming more structured and disciplined. I did shadow work, breathwork, energy work, hypnotherapy; studied personality types; meditated daily; went on spiritual retreats; followed spiritual masters; and researched ancient religions.

You name it, I've probably tried it. I was desperate to stop my own suffering. Although some of these things did help me—and they've likely helped you too—they didn't end my suffering. I still felt anxious, fearful, unfulfilled, irritated, angry, and frustrated every day. Even after trying everything, I didn't feel any closer to a solution, and if I'm being honest, I felt even more hopeless than when I had begun. I didn't know what to do anymore, where to look, or who to talk to. It wasn't until I was in my darkest hour that a glimmer of hope began to lead me to the light.

Suddenly, after years of searching, I stumbled upon a concept that took me right back to the teaching of the two arrows and how I could prevent the second one from hitting so I didn't have to suffer emotionally anymore.

The answer was in understanding how our minds work and how the human experience is created.

how long are you going to keep holding on
to the story you don't want to keep reliving?

Chapter 2

The Root Cause of Suffering

One who looks around him is intelligent;
one who looks within him is wise.

—MATSHONA DHLIWAYO

We live in a world of thought, not reality. Philosopher Sydney Banks once said, "Thought is not reality, yet it is through thought that our realities are created." What he means by this is that each of us lives through our own perception of the world, which is vastly different from that of the person next to us.

For example, you could be sitting in a coffee shop having an existential crisis, completely stressed out of your mind about how you have no idea what you're doing with your life, while at the same time, the person next to you is happily enjoying their freshly brewed drink and peacefully people-watching.

You are both in the same coffee shop, smelling the same aromas, surrounded by the same strangers, but how the world looks to each of you couldn't be more different. Many of us go through the same events in exactly the same locations at the same time, yet we are having radically different experiences of the world. This is what I mean when I say that we live in a world of thought and not reality.

Reality is what is happening right now. It is the objective circumstance that is occurring without any meaning or judgment attached to it. And so what we experience is not reality itself but our *perception* of reality. Any meaning or thinking we give something is self-created and our choice.

Here's another example: if you walk up to one hundred different people and ask each of them what money means to them, how many different answers do you think you'll get?

Money has a technical definition, but it *means* something different to each of us. Depending on who you are, money could mean time, freedom, opportunity, security, and peace of mind, or it could mean evil, greed, and the basis for crimes. There are no right or wrong answers here, but the meaning we give something is the filter through which we see life.

Just imagine how many answers you'll get if you ask one hundred people their opinions on the current president. Even though it's the same person we're talking about, you will get quite a few different answers because we all have different beliefs we are projecting onto what we are observing.

This is where we return to the idea of the two arrows: pain and suffering. It's not the events that happen in our lives but our *interpretation* of them that causes us to feel good or bad. This is how people in developing countries can be happier than people in developed countries and how people in developed countries can be more miserable than people in developing countries.

Our feelings come not from external events but from our own *thinking* about the events.

Let's hypothetically say that you really hate your job and that it causes you an enormous amount of stress. It pains you to even set foot in the building where you work, and just thinking about your job makes you anxious. Even when you're at home with your family, sitting on the sofa and watching a TV show together, you're completely occupied thinking about how miserable your job makes you. Everyone else on that sofa is having a good time except for you.

At this moment, the rest of your family is having an experience of life that is different from yours, even though the same event—watching TV—is happening for all of you. Just thinking about work is creating a whole different perception of reality for you, even though you are not physically at work.

If it were true that external events are solely responsible for internal feelings, then you would be a happy camper in your living room, enjoying the moment every time you watch a funny TV show with your loved ones. But that's not the case.

Now, you may say that you're only feeling unhappy because a negative external circumstance, your job, is causing you stress. To that, I'll ask, While a job may be demanding, does that mean it must lead to suffering?

Or put another way, Is it absolutely true that every person who has the same intense job feels the exact same way about that job?

Take paramedics or firefighters, for example. While their jobs can be very intense, not every person working those jobs has the same experience of it. Some may experience anxiety, dread, and distress, while others experience calm, fulfillment, and even excitement.

Two people can be doing the same job but have very different experiences of it. It can be the most amazing dream job for one person but the other person's worst nightmare. The question is, What determines which experience someone will have?

Let's do a quick thought experiment to see.

Consider again the theoretically stressful job, the one that you hate. **How would you feel if you didn't *think* that you hated your job?**

Take a few moments to see what comes up for you.

If you don't overthink it and simply let the answers surface from within you, I imagine you will come to the conclusion that without that line of *thinking*—the ruminating, judging, and spiraling—you would most likely feel peaceful, free, and light. Even if you didn't change anything about the job itself.

Which means that without our usual *thinking* about a particular event, our experience of it completely alters.

And with this understanding, we've arrived at the truth I discovered after all those years of searching:

The root cause of our suffering is our own thinking.

Before you light this book on fire and throw it across the room, please know I'm not saying that what we are experiencing isn't real. Our *perception of reality* is very real. We feel what we think, and our emotions are real. That is undeniable. However, what I *am* saying is that how we feel will look like an inevitable, unchangeable reality until we recognize the role that our thinking plays in creating it. By changing our thinking, we can change our reality. And if that is true, then we are only ever one thought away from transforming our lives and letting go of our suffering.

In short, the moment we stop thinking is when our happiness begins.

The Human Experience Equation

Our experience of reality is created from the combination of the events we encounter and what we think about them. To reiterate, our emotions come not from external events but from our thinking about them.

Here is a more visual way to understand how our thinking can change our experience of an event through a simple equation:

Event + Same thinking = Same experience

Event + New thinking = New experience

What this equation means is that when we go through an event and think about it the same way we always have, it will always produce the same experience and therefore the same emotion. But if we change our thinking about that same event, we can alter our experience of it and create a new emotional response.

When you change your thinking, you change your experience of life—*without* needing to change the event that happened.

However, while we can change our thinking, the most ideal path to serenity is to let go of our thinking entirely. Without our own thinking about an event, we find peace because we are experiencing exactly what reality is without our own judgments, stories, or expectations of it. If we simplify the equation, we can see exactly this:

Event + Thinking = Perception of reality

Event without thinking = Reality

Event without thinking = Peace

*   *   *

A Young Monk and the Empty Boat: A Zen Story about How Our Thinking Is the Cause of Our Suffering

A long time ago, a young Zen monk lived in a small monastery in a forest near a lake. A few senior monks occupied the monastery, while the rest were newcomers who still had much to learn. The monks had many duties. One of the most important parts of their daily routine was when they had to sit down, close their eyes, and meditate in silence for hours at a time.

After each meditation, they had to report their progress to their mentor. One young monk had difficulty staying focused during his meditation practice for various reasons, which made him very angry. After the young monk reported his progress to his mentor, the elder asked a simple question with a hidden lesson:

"Do you know what is really making you angry?"

The young monk replied, "Well, as soon as I close my eyes and meditate, someone starts moving around, and I can't focus. I get agitated that someone is disturbing me even though they know that I'm meditating. How can they not be more considerate? And then, when I close my eyes again and try to focus, a cat or a small animal might brush past and disturb me again. By this point, even when the wind blows and the tree branches make a noise, I get angry. If that is not enough, the birds keep on chirping, and I can't seem to find any peace in this place."

The elder monk simply pointed out to his pupil, "I see that you become angrier with each interruption you encounter. This is exactly the opposite of the point of meditating. You should find a way not to get angry with people, animals, or anything around you that disturbs you during your task."

After their consultation, the young monk left the monastery and looked around to find a place that would be quieter so that he could meditate peacefully. He found such a place at the shore of the lake nearby. He brought his mat, sat down, and started meditating. But soon, a flock of birds splashed down in the lake. Hearing their noise, the monk opened his eyes in rage.

Even though the bank of the lake was quieter than the monastery, things were still disturbing his peace, and he got angry again. But even though he didn't find the peace he was looking for, he kept returning to the lake. Then one day, the monk saw a boat tied to the end of a small pier. "Why don't I take the boat, row it down to the middle of the lake, and meditate there?" he thought. "In the middle of the lake, there will be nothing to disturb me!" He rowed the boat to the middle of the lake and started meditating.

As he had expected, there was nothing in the middle of the lake to disturb him, and he was able to meditate the whole day. At the end of the day, he returned to the monastery. This continued for a few days, and the monk was thrilled that he had finally found a place to meditate in peace. He didn't feel angry and could calmly continue the meditation practice.

Then one day, when the monk was meditating in the middle of the lake, he heard water splashing and felt the boat rocking. He started getting upset that even in the middle of the lake, someone was disturbing him.

Opening his eyes, he saw a boat heading straight toward him. He shouted, "Steer your boat away, or you will hit my boat!" But the other boat kept coming directly at him and was only a few feet away. He yelled again, but there was no response, and the incoming boat hit the monk's boat. Now he was furious. "Who are you, and why have you hit my boat in the middle of this vast lake?" he screamed. There was no answer. This made him even angrier.

He stood up to see who was in the other boat, and to his surprise, *he found no one in the boat.*

The boat had probably come untied and drifted along in the breeze until it had bumped into the monk's boat. It was just an empty boat! The monk found his anger dissipating, for there was no one to get angry at.

At that moment, he remembered his mentor's question: "Do you know what is really making you angry?" Now he knew he had his answer. "It's not other people, situations, or circumstances. It's not the empty boat but my reaction to it that causes my anger.

All the people or situations that upset me are like the empty boat. Without my reaction, they don't have the power to make me angry."

The monk then rowed the boat back to the shore. He returned to the monastery and started meditating along with the others. There were still noises and disturbances, but he treated them as empty boats and continued meditating peacefully. When the elder monk saw the difference, he said to the young monk, "I see that you have found what is really making you angry and you have overcome that."

true freedom
isn't in having complete control of our minds
but in the ability to be unattached
   to whatever happens in it

Chapter 3

Why Do We Think?

I think and think and think, I've thought myself out of happiness one million times, but never once into it.

—JONATHAN SAFRAN FOER

As humans, we have evolved with a sophisticated ability to rationalize, analyze, and think because these are key to our survival.

The mind's job is to alert us to potential dangers in our environment that may threaten our lives. It does its job so well that not only will it scan our immediate surroundings for threats, but it will even reference past experiences to create predictions of possible future dangers based on our memories.

None of this is wrong by any means. The mind is simply doing what it was designed to do. But while our minds do an incredible job of keeping us alive, this same ability does not allow us to thrive.

For instance, in prehistoric times, many things— animals, weather, illness—were a threat to our existence.

We survived because of our ability to communicate, work together, form strong social bonds, and pass down knowledge from one generation to the next. It was vital to stay in our social groups, and being thrown out of our tribe meant certain death.

And so our minds evolved to fear being judged or doing the wrong thing in order to remain accepted by others and not get kicked out of the tribe. Because of this, we sacrificed our individuality and uniqueness to fit in. We learned to not be too different or weird because it might result in us being ostracized. While this may have helped us survive, it also cost us our peace and happiness.

Although our brains are still hardwired this way, we no longer live in a world where social acceptance means life and death. Losing a social bond may be painful, but it no longer means we have to fend for ourselves in the wild.

Today, the question isn't whether we will survive but whether we are happy with the time we are alive. Our quality of life is determined by the peace, fulfillment, and joy we feel on a daily basis.

And yet there is a mismatch because we are navigating today's world with a mind that is still programmed with this primitive fear. The problem is that we often forget this distinction. Our mind's duty is to keep us alive. Our consciousness's duty is to help us feel fulfilled. Our soul is the reason why we're even on this journey in the first place—to find peace within ourselves.

If we keep allowing this thinking to direct our lives, we will stay in a state of fight or flight, anxiety, fear, frustration, depression, anger, resentment, and negative emotion because the mind views everything as a threat to our very existence. And it is this tendency of our minds that leads us to the torturous thinking at the root of our suffering.

If you want to be free and at peace, then you will need to let go of only listening to your mind's fight-or-flight thinking. You are not just a product of your environment but a co-creator of it. With this understanding, you can begin to shift your experience of reality from merely surviving to truly thriving.

the path to self-actualization
isn't to try to improve ourselves
    because we think we're not enough
but to let go of the illusion
that we're not already enough as we are

Chapter 4

Thoughts versus Thinking

Stop thinking and end your problems.
—LAO TZU

Thoughts are the energetic, mental raw materials our minds use to understand and navigate the world. Thoughts are neutral observations, insights, or intuitive promptings that pop into our minds. A thought takes little to no effort to produce; it's something that just happens. The flip side of this is that we also cannot always control what thoughts enter our minds.

Thinking, on the other hand, is the judgment or opinion we have about our thoughts. Thinking takes a significant amount of energy, effort, and willpower, which are finite resources. You don't have to ruminate on each thought that enters your mind, but when you do, that is thinking.

A simple way to recall the distinction between thoughts and thinking is to remember that *thought* is a noun and isn't something that we do but something we *have*. Thinking, on the other hand, is a verb and is something we *do*. It is the act of *engaging* with our thoughts.

Let's do a quick thought experiment to explore this difference.

What is something you've been dreaming about doing but haven't done yet?

Pause here and wait for an answer to surface.

Sit with the initial thought of what you want to do and become aware of how it makes you feel.

Now let's dig deeper. What would it take to make that dream a reality? What are the reasons you have or haven't done it yet? What is holding you back from making it happen?

How do these further questions make you feel? Sit with those emotions and see what comes up for you.

Now let's review what happened.

When I asked you what you dreamed about doing, your answer was a *thought*. If it truly was a dream of yours, then initially, you likely felt inspired, expansive, and excited by it.

Then I asked you to think further about your answer, to consider what it would take to make it happen and what is holding you back. After thinking about those questions, did you notice a shift in energy?

You likely felt heavier, disappointed, frustrated, and maybe even a bit fearful. The answers were probably more judgmental and negative compared to your initial answer of what you wanted to do.

You may have been thinking about how it's impossible, how you could fail, what other people might think of you, how you're not good enough to do it, or how it's just a pipe dream.

If this exercise did not bring up anything negative for you, that is okay. The purpose of the thought experiment was to help you identify the moment a thought shifts to thinking and rumination. We all have different scenarios that prompt this for us, so if this one didn't resonate with you, you can create your own thought experiment by recalling a situation that caused you to overthink and identifying the initial neutral thought and the subsequent thinking that caused emotional suffering.

Thoughts are intrinsically neutral. But the moment we begin thinking about our thoughts, we get taken on an emotional roller coaster. This is what I mean when I say that thinking is the root of our suffering. The initial thought of your dream didn't cause any suffering until you began *thinking* about the thought.

The good news is that it is not necessary to think about our thoughts or judge them. We may believe that thinking is useful, but it's an illusion that causes us to experience negative, unwanted emotions.

The only useful and helpful thing was the initial thought that popped into your mind when I first asked what you dreamed of doing. All of the thinking that happened after was destructive and unhelpful.

To help illustrate this idea, take a look at the following scenarios. In each, notice the difference between the initial reaction—the thought—and the negative rumination that occurs when one begins thinking about the thought.

Situation:

An event

Thought	Thinking
Neutral observation or intuitive prompting	Negative judgment or story about the thought

Situation:

It is raining.

Thought	Thinking
It is raining.	Why does this always happen to me?
	This is the worst.
	This ruined my day.

Situation:

You lost your job.

Thought	Thinking
I lost my job.	I'm not good enough.
	Everyone is judging me.
	I'll never recover from this.
	This is unfair.

Situation:

You arrive at work and find it unfulfilling.

Thought	Thinking
I want to quit my job.	What if I can't find another job?
	I might hate the next job even more.
	I'm not good enough to get another job.
	Why would anyone hire me?

Situation:

It is the weekend and you are deciding what to do.

Thought	Thinking
I want to start a new creative hobby.	It's a waste of time.
	I'm not creative.
	I'm not good at it.
	Other people are going to judge me.

Thoughts create. Thinking destroys.

As soon as we begin to think about our thoughts, we cast our own limiting beliefs, judgments, criticisms, programming, and conditioning onto them.

Without the step of thinking, we can prevent all negative programming and judgments from tarnishing the initial thought of what we want to create.

So what do thoughts look like without thinking? To return to our experiment, if I asked you to think of some ways you could make your dream a reality, if you sat there long enough, you would experience the same phenomenon of having spontaneous thoughts pop into your head of ways you could make it happen.

These are thoughts of creation. Thoughts have the quality of being infinite and expansive and of feeling energetically aligned with you. They make you feel excited, lighter, and alive.

As soon as you begin thinking about your thoughts, you'll immediately feel heavy, restricted, and limited, along with a cascade of negative emotions. This is how you'll know you're thinking.

Our emotions are an internal radar system that tells us if we are experiencing thoughts or have fallen into the trap of thinking.

What follows is a chart that compares different attributes of thoughts and thinking to help you identify which one is which within your mind. Try going through a few examples of thoughts you've had today, and use the chart to check if what you experienced was a thought or if it was thinking.

Thoughts versus Thinking

Attribute	Thought	Thinking
Source	Universe	Ego
Charge	Neutral	Negative
Weight	Light	Heavy
Energy	Expansive	Restrictive
Nature	Infinite	Limited
Quality	Creative	Destructive
Essence	Divine	Mortal
Feeling	Alive	Stressful
Emotion	Love	Fear
Sense	Wholeness	Separateness
Effort	Effortless	Laborious
Root	Truth	Illusion
Time	Present	Past/Future

questioning your own thinking creates

s   p   a   c   e

for new thoughts

   to change your life

Chapter 5

But Don't We Need to Think Positively?

Our most natural state is joy. It is the foundation for love, compassion, healing, and the desire to alleviate suffering.

—DEEPAK CHOPRA

You may be wondering, If thinking creates negative emotions, can I completely remove negative emotions from my life by stopping thinking? Is that even something I should want?

While decreasing our thinking is key to reducing our suffering, our goal isn't necessarily to stop feeling negative emotions altogether. Some of these emotions can be helpful, such as fear when walking down a dark alley alone with no one else in sight. Or unhappiness letting you know it's time to leave behind a relationship that is no longer serving you. These emotions serve as guidance to help us create better circumstances and environments for nurturing our growth.

However, dwelling in a state of fear or negativity when there is no immediate threat to our survival is more harmful than helpful. The goal is to decrease the amount of time it takes for us to regulate our emotions and return to a state of peace when we experience something stressful. This will enable us to decrease the suffering caused by thinking as much as possible.

When I mention that thinking leads to negative emotions, most people assume that we must therefore have positive thoughts or think positively in order to feel positive emotions. But this is not the case. While positive thoughts can lead to positive emotions, it is not the only way to experience them, nor is it required.

Let's investigate further with this question:

Throughout your life, have you felt joy only when you've had positive thoughts?

Of course not! It would be *exhausting* if we had to constantly recall happy memories, imagine an ideal future, or list everything we're grateful for every second of the day just to feel joy. We would drive ourselves crazy, and it simply isn't sustainable. It would be difficult to function because most of our time would be spent thinking about our lives instead of actually living them.

The truth is that you do not have to have thoughts or think to feel positive emotions. Positive emotions are not a byproduct of thinking but the organic result of being fully in the present moment and connected to life rather than thinking about it.

These feelings we desire are already within us. We don't have to try to force them. We only don't feel them when we begin thinking and separating ourselves from this source.

Why? Because our natural state of being *is* joy, love, and peace. This may be hard to believe because if it's natural, then wouldn't we always feel that way?

If we want to see the natural state of something, one of the best ways is to look at its state of infancy, before it's affected and conditioned by its environment.

To understand our natural state, let's consider that of a child. What is a child's natural, default state? Are they naturally stressed, anxious, fearful, and self-conscious? Or are they mostly in a state of bliss, happiness, and love?

Children are innately open, curious, happy, and full of wonder and laughter. This is also the natural state of adults until we think ourselves out of it.

Whenever you feel highly stressed, you will notice that you have a significant amount of thinking going on. The strength of the negative emotion you feel is directly proportional to how much thinking you are doing in the moment.

On the other hand, the intensity of the positive emotion you feel is inversely proportional to the amount of thinking you are doing at the moment. In other words, the less thinking you have going on, the stronger the positive emotion you feel in the present.

To see the truth in this, recall a recent time when you were highly stressed and anxious. How much thinking were you doing then?

Quite a lot, right?

Now recall a time when you were really happy. How much thinking were you doing at the time?

Most likely none or very little.

Now how do you feel when you're not thinking?

Take a few moments to see what comes up for you.

If you don't overthink it and simply let the answers surface from within you, you will realize that when you're not thinking, you experience calm, peace, or even joy.

This is the secret to your serenity.

An analogy to help visualize this concept is to imagine our minds have speedometers (like in a car), but instead of speed, it measures the amount of thinking. The more thinking we have going on, the higher the "think-o-meter" goes, and if we have enough thinking going on, it'll go into the red zone. This is when we feel stressed, burned out, frustrated, and angry.

It's not *what* we're thinking about that is causing us suffering but *that* we are thinking.

The only time we don't naturally feel at peace are when we begin to think about the thoughts we're having, thereby blocking our direct connection to the present. Thinking takes us away from the present moment and into the past or future, which are the only times regret or anxiety exist. You do not have to "try" to be present or "think positively" to experience love, joy, bliss, or any other positive emotions because those emotions *are* our natural state when we are not thinking. More times than not, the solution to our problems is not the addition of action but the removal of what's causing those problems in the first place.

most of us are chasing external things
so that we can feel something inside
   innocently forgetting that all feelings are
       generated within us

what is external
   is only a reminder
that we can create
   the internal emotion we desire

what you most want to experience
   can only be found within you

don't wait for something outside of you
to give you permission
   to feel how you want inside

Chapter 6

How Do We Stop Thinking?

A crowded mind leaves no space for a peaceful heart.
—CHRISTINE EVANGELOU

Heaven and Hell: A Zen Parable

A tough, brawny samurai once approached a Zen master deep in meditation. Impatient and discourteous, the samurai demanded in his husky voice so accustomed to forceful yelling, "Tell me the nature of heaven and hell!"

The Zen master opened his eyes, looked the samurai in the face, and replied with scorn, "Why should I answer to a shabby, disgusting, despondent slob like you? A worm like you, do you think I should tell you anything? I can't stand you. Get out of my sight. I have no time for silly questions."

The samurai could not bear these insults. Consumed by rage, he drew his sword and raised it to sever the master's head at once.

Looking straight into the samurai's eyes, the Zen master tenderly declared, "That's hell."

The samurai froze. He immediately understood that anger had him in its grip. His mind had just created his own hell—one filled with resentment, hatred, self-defense, and fury. He realized that he was so deep in his torment that he was ready to kill somebody.

The samurai's eyes filled with tears. Setting his sword aside, he put his palms together and bowed in gratitude for this insight.

The Zen master gently acknowledged with a delicate smile, "And that's heaven."

*   *   *

While letting go of our thinking is the key to ending our suffering, this doesn't necessarily mean that our goal should be to stop thinking entirely. Just as the goal is not to stop feeling negative emotions entirely. That would be impractical and nearly impossible. The goal is to minimize the time we spend thinking about our thoughts so that eventually, we can get to the point where we spend most of our day not caught up in our thinking and live in a harmonious state more often.

But how do we do this?

This may surprise you, but we don't have to *do* anything to minimize our thinking; we only have to become aware of it and choose to let it go rather than hold on to it. Most of us have been conditioned to "fight" our thinking, which only worsens things and leads to the agonizing experience we call "overthinking." The solution is not about doing *more* but about *not* doing what's causing the suffering. It is not a process of force but one of flow.

By becoming aware that we are thinking and that it is the root cause of suffering, we can detach from it, allowing it to settle and pass. While it may seem counterintuitive, the best way to end overthinking and negative feelings is to stop resisting and avoiding them. What we resist persists. What we accept and let be will inevitably leave.

Here's an analogy that illustrates this concept.

Imagine I give you a bowl of cloudy, dirty, murky water. If I asked you how you would make the water clear, how would you do it?

Wait to see what answers arise before moving on.

Most people say something like filtering the water or even boiling it. What most people don't realize is that if we let the bowl of dirty water sit for a period of time, the dirt will begin to settle on its own in the water, and after a while, the water will become clear on its own.

This is how our minds work as well. If we let our thinking sit without disturbing it by trying to fight it—our internal version of filtering and boiling—the thinking will settle down on its own, and our minds will become free from thinking. The natural state of water is clear, and the natural state of the mind is also clear if we do not disturb it.

If life begins to feel unclear, disorganized, and stressful, and you're not sure what to do next, it's only because your thinking is stirring up the dirt, making your mind cloudy and making it difficult to see ahead. When you sense this cloudiness, see it as an indicator that you're thinking too much. Then allow your thinking to settle by acknowledging it and giving it space to pass without judgment, and slowly, the mind will clear again.

We can also compare thinking to quicksand. The more we fight our thinking, the more we get caught up in it, amplifying our negative emotions and worsening them. The same is true for quicksand. If we're in quicksand, the way out isn't to fight it. If we panic and frantically try to fight it, we only get pulled under faster. The only way out is to stop struggling and allow the body's natural buoyancy to take over and bring us back to the surface easily.

The way to break free from our thinking is to relax our minds and trust that our natural inner wisdom will guide us back to clarity and peace like it always has.

If you find yourself fluctuating between thinking and non-thinking, know that it is absolutely okay and quite normal. There is no way we can remain in a state of non-thinking every second of every day. And if we try to make that the goal, we will only end up battling our minds, ending up in a cycle of thinking again and causing ourselves to suffer.

We are spiritual, infinite beings having a physical, finite experience here on earth. Because of this, we are a living gateway between the human and the divine, so we will naturally oscillate between the states of feeling anxious/stressed and joyful/peaceful. We cannot always control or prevent the oscillation between thinking and non-thinking, but we can minimize the time spent thinking and thus create more moments where we feel joyful, peaceful, passionate, and full of love.

Although not being able to control when we begin thinking or experiencing stress can feel frustrating, it is not something to worry about because we can always return to the state of non-thinking or serenity. It is just a part of our beautiful human experience.

What can give us true peace is knowing that we always have this state of pure peace, love, and fulfillment lying underneath any suffering we are experiencing.

This beautiful state is not something we ever lose, but only forget. And just because we can sometimes forget about it doesn't mean it's not there. Just like how we know the sun still exists even when it's dark.

We are only ever one moment away from remembering that we always have in our possession an infinite well of clarity, love, joy, and peace.

If we find ourselves overthinking and ruminating again, all we have to do is remember that this is just our temporary thinking and find solace in knowing that the sun will rise again soon enough. Having that understanding will also allow us to appreciate the nighttime for its existence and role in the universe. From that, we can see how it is meant to be a part of our human experience and begin to cherish its beauty as much as the sun.

thoughts are transient
they come and go
   but **You** always stay

if you want to know who you are
look beyond your thoughts
to experience your true nature

Chapter 7

Practical Steps for How to Stop Thinking

I swear to you that to think too much is a disease, a real, actual disease.

—FYODOR DOSTOYEVSKY

Learning to overcome our thinking may be simple, but it is not always easy. Becoming aware of our emotional states and letting go of our painful thinking patterns without fighting them will take practice.

If you are still struggling with how to stop thinking, it is okay. Do not beat yourself up over it. What we need most during difficult times is not more self-criticism but more love, compassion, and patience for ourselves.

Here is a simple five-step process to help you let go of your thinking, which you'll notice conveniently spells out the acronym PAUSE.

The first step is to **pause** and begin taking deep breaths to help calm our nervous systems. Deep breaths pull our focus away from the thinking mind and into our bodies, anchoring us in the present moment. This allows us to become aware of our emotions and also detach from them.

Pausing creates space between our emotions and actions, giving us the opportunity to *choose* a new response rather than repeating the same conditioned reactions that keep us in the cycle of suffering. Without this space, change cannot exist. Space has the illusion of emptiness on the surface. It is not empty but filled with infinite possibilities for us to choose a new experience of life. Within the space between your thoughts and your thinking lies the peace you've been seeking.

Step two is to **ask** yourself, "Is this thinking making me feel the way I want?" or "Do I want to keep suffering?" These questions remind us of the power we have to choose whether we want to emotionally suffer or not. If we want to keep feeling the way we do, then we can choose to do so. We've all had times when we are not yet ready to let the negativity pass, and that is okay. But if we want peace, we can choose it by letting go of the thinking that is causing our suffering.

Step three is to **understand** that you have the *choice* to stop and let go of your thinking. At this moment, you must decide what you want. Is it peace, or is it to continue the thinking that is causing the suffering? This can be scary, but if you trust yourself and that you will be okay no matter what happens, it becomes easier to let go.

Step four is to **say** and repeat to yourself, "Thinking is the root cause of suffering." Reminding yourself of this disempowers your thinking, making it easier to manage because you begin to see through it. Repeating this phrase to yourself like a mantra when you begin experiencing negative emotions is a powerful practice. It is difficult for our minds to have multiple thoughts simultaneously, so repeating a single phrase forces the brain to focus only on it rather than something else. The reason mantras are effective is not just because of the power of words to influence our beliefs but because they reduce or even stop our minds from thinking.

Step five is to **experience** your emotions fully. Most of our destructive habits and behaviors come from the avoidance and suppression of emotions. When we ignore or fight our feelings, we only make our suffering worse. We are not trying to bypass our emotions. Rather, we are trying to accept and feel them fully without judgment. Suffering comes not from our emotions but from the thinking we attach to the emotions.

What would it feel like to experience your emotions without judgment? Can you feel how there's less resistance to them? Can you feel how much easier it is to let them go? How much more liberating does that feel?

We unnecessarily create our own suffering by trying to make our minds do jobs they are not designed to do. Your mind's job is to anticipate threats. Your body's job is to regulate the resulting emotions. Everything has a role. When you let your body feel and process emotions fully without the interference of your judgmental thinking, emotions will naturally pass more easily and quickly than you realize. The mind and body will always restore balance and harmony naturally when we get out of the way.

How to Let Go of Negative Thinking: PAUSE

To help you remember this five-step process more easily, use the acronym PAUSE. It spells out the steps for letting go of your thinking. Whenever you're feeling overwhelmed by your thinking, *pause*, go through the five steps, and remember that you have the power to let go of it at any time.

P—Pause and take deep breaths to calm your nervous system and ground yourself in the present. Become aware that you are thinking, but do not judge it.

A—Ask yourself, "Is this thinking making me feel the way I want?" or "Do I want to keep suffering?" If not, you always have the choice to let your thinking go in order to find peace.

U—Understand that you have the choice to stop and let go of it.

S—Say and repeat the mantra "Thinking is the root cause of suffering" to help quiet the mind from thinking until it subsides and passes.

E—Experience your emotions fully without judgment, resistance, or thinking (don't think; just feel).

Repeat this process until you have calmed your nervous system and the thinking has passed.

One of the most effective ways to make this a sustainable and permanent change is to use negative emotions as a reminder that you are thinking. Then go through this process of letting go to return to a state of peace. It is important to do this throughout the day so that you minimize the amount of time you spend thinking about your thoughts, allowing you to remain in a state of peace and love longer. As with learning anything new, it is always more difficult in the beginning, but it becomes easier each time you practice it. When you have been practicing this long enough, it will become second nature to you, and peace will become your primary state of being rather than stress. This is the single most important practice you can make for your peace.

You may be wondering, though, about whether any other actions can help us heal and ease mental suffering. Most modalities designed to help people reduce anxiety do work. Therapy, yoga, meditation, breathwork, and anything similar all have been proven to lower stress levels, but why do many people still suffer even when utilizing them?

As I mentioned at the beginning of the book, I explored these interventions but still felt emotional turmoil. To understand why, let's dig into the specifics.

Let's take meditation as an example. When I meditated in the morning, the session felt wonderful, and I was able to feel more at peace during the practice. But within an hour or even minutes after, all of the anxiety would come rushing back. Fifteen minutes of meditation for only fifteen minutes of peace did not seem like a great investment. The benefits of these practices did not outlast the practice. I was so frustrated because almost everything I tried had similar results.

Then I asked myself, "What is happening during these practices that allows me to experience peace?"

This is when a lightbulb went on in my head. What was happening during the practice was that I wasn't thinking. But as soon as the session ended, I began thinking again, which is why all of the anxiety came back shortly after. It wasn't that the modality didn't work; rather, I was not addressing the root of the problem, so my thinking would always return and prevent the modality from continuing to work.

As soon as I shifted from only letting go of thinking during healing practices to doing so throughout my day, everything changed. Slowly but surely, my days started shifting from being anxious and stressful most of the time to being peaceful the majority of the day. This transformed a practice that only worked while I was doing it into a state of being I could experience in every moment.

So as to the question of whether these modalities can help, they very much can! However, they are most effective when viewed as tools to expand our awareness and help us practice letting go of our thinking.

The important thing to recognize is that we need to take with us the non-thinking skills we learn during these other practices and continue to use them throughout the day.

The concept of non-thinking is meant not to replace any practice you currently have but to complement, enhance, and prolong the effects of what you already do.

one of the greatest powers we possess is *choice*

Chapter 8

How Can We Possibly Thrive in the World without Thinking?

Anxiety is thought without control.
Flow is control without thought.

—JAMES CLEAR

Now that you've come to the realization that thinking is the root cause of suffering, you may be wondering, *How can I possibly thrive in the world without thinking?* To answer that question, let's consider a different one: What thoughts are going through your head when you're doing your absolute best work—when you're fully captivated and entranced by what you're doing in the moment?

Take a moment and see what answer comes up for you.

If you still haven't had any insight from an answer, here's another question that may help: When you love what you do and are so completely immersed in it that you lose all sense of time and space (in other words, enter a flow state), how much thinking is going on at that moment?

Pause here and wait for the answer to arise.

Isn't that an interesting phenomenon? When you're doing your best work and are in a total state of flow, where there is no separation between you and the work you are doing, little to no thinking is happening in the mind. Your self-judgmental chatter is minimal or even silent. And if you have thoughts, they are neutral, constructive, or creative. They aid you in the activity you are engaged in and flow right through you without you having to think about them. In other words, the state of peak performance for humans can be described as the state of non-thinking. It may come as a surprise to you, but we do our best work when we aren't thinking.

Here's another example that illustrates this idea from another perspective. When professional athletes are competing, do you think they are thinking and overanalyzing every single thing that's happening during the game? How much thinking do you imagine is going on during the competition for them? The highest-performing athletes will describe their peak state as being in "the zone." This "zone" is the state of flow or non-thinking. I use both terms in this book; know that they are interchangeable.

In Japanese culture, there is a beautiful word to describe this phenomenon: *mushin*, which is often translated as "no mind."

Here is the definition of *mushin* in practice from the *Shotokan Times*:

> Mushin is achieved when [the] mind is free of random thoughts, free of anger, free of fear, and particularly free of ego. It applies during combat and/or other facets of life. When mushin is achieved during combat, there is an absence of loose or rambling thoughts. It leaves the practitioner free to act and react without hesitation. He reacts according to all of the study and training that has brought [him] to this point. Relying on not what you think should be your next move but on what your trained, instinctive, subconscious reaction directs you to do.

After practice, thinking hinders the performance of athletes, and the same is true for everyone. We only hesitate, are reluctant, and have doubts when we begin thinking and overanalyzing. We function and perform our best and embody our full potential when we enter a state of non-thinking.

Because there is no separation when we are in a flow state, we can also say that it is a state where we are in direct connection and alignment with the Universe/God/Infinite Intelligence.

Thinking blocks this connection we have with the divine, causing us to feel stress, frustration, anger, resentment, depression, and all of these negative emotions many of us feel daily. This is why some religions describe hell as a complete separation from God.

Many attribute the state of non-thinking or flow to a particular activity that we love to do, which creates a misconception that that's the only time we can be in flow. This is only half true. We can be in a state of non-thinking at any point in time as long as we are rooted in the present moment.

Only in the present moment can the truth be found. This is why mindfulness instructors, spiritual masters, and even therapists share the importance of meditation, breathing, and being in the present moment. In the Bible, when Moses asks God His name, He replies, "I am." God doesn't say He *was* or *will be*, because those don't exist in the now. He simply says, "I am." God, truth, the Universe, freedom, peace, joy, and love (these terms are all synonymous) can only be found, and therefore experienced, in the present.

In a state of flow, grounded in the present moment, we are free from the limitations of the ego and can create the most incredible things in the world.

you cannot think your way into flow
just as much as you cannot think your way
    into love

both are a natural occurrence
when we let go
and allow the full authentic expression of
    ourselves to come forth

they are a byproduct
    of surrender and trust

Chapter 9

What about Our Goals, Dreams, and Ambitions?

*There are no limitations to the mind
except those we acknowledge.*

—NAPOLEON HILL

I think, therefore I suffer.

When I finally realized that thinking was the root cause of my suffering, it was a huge epiphany for me. I felt exhilarated, relieved, and grateful that I had discovered the true reason for my negative experiences. This ecstasy was short lived, though, because soon after the exuberance settled, the following questions popped into my mind:

If thinking is the root cause of all my suffering and I stop thinking, how do I live my life now? What about all of my goals, dreams, and ambitions? Do I need to stop wanting things in life? Will I devolve

into a couch potato and not do anything meaningful with my life?

As I pondered these questions, fear and anxiety
began to surface because it seemed that in order to
find peace and happiness, I would have to give up
all my dreams and become a monk in the middle of
the mountains.

I was not ready to do that, nor did I want to. As
much as detaching from my life might have made
my journey easier, I genuinely enjoyed being in the
world and experiencing the fullness of life with other
people.

So what are we to do if we wish to end our suffering but also not give up the lives we have built?
To answer that question, let's return to the concept of
thoughts versus thinking. As we discussed previously,
each has a different source: thoughts come from the
universe or our higher selves, while thinking comes
from our own egos. The source dictates whether it
causes suffering or not.

Similarly, where our goals and dreams come from
will determine how we feel pursuing them. The key is
understanding the difference.

**There are two sources of goals: goals created out
of inspiration and goals created out of desperation.**

When goals are created out of desperation, we
feel an immense sense of scarcity and urgency. They feel
heavy, like a burden, and we may feel daunted by

the colossal task we've just committed ourselves to. Impostor syndrome and self-doubt begin to manifest, and we feel like we're always short on time. We go about our lives frantically, desperately searching for ways to accomplish our goals faster, always looking externally to fill the void we feel internally.

Worst of all, if we achieve the goal, soon after, all those feelings of lack begin to resurface again. We start feeling discontented with what we've done, unable to savor our accomplishments, and because what we did never feels like it's enough, we feel that same way about ourselves. Not knowing what else to do, we look at what others are doing for guidance and see that they're continuing to do the same thing. Thus, we proceed to set another goal out of desperation in an attempt to escape all of the negative feelings gnawing away at our souls.

When we dig a little deeper into these types of desperation goals, we see they are all typically "means goals" and not "end goals." In other words, we want to accomplish the goal in order to get something else, which is why these goals make us feel that we never have enough. An example of this would be having a goal of becoming famous in order to finally feel significant. Unless you address the internal root worry that you're not good enough, achieving this external goal will never change how you feel.

Ironically, if we achieve a goal created out of desperation, we end up feeling even emptier than before, so we set an even bigger goal and then an even bigger one, never reaching a state of fulfillment. No matter how hard we try or how big of a goal we set, it seems as though it will never be enough.

If you have experienced this, know that you are not alone. This is how most of us set our goals and live our lives. The only reason I can describe it in such detail is that this was how I lived my life as well.

Here's the good news: it's not your fault if you set goals that way—it's what so many of us have been taught to do—and there's a way out through creating goals and dreams out of inspiration instead of desperation.

When we create goals out of inspiration, it's an entirely different story. In this state, we are creating because we feel deeply moved, inspired, and expansive. Our goals feel like a calling rather than an obligation. We feel like a powerful force of life is coming from within us, wanting to be expressed through us and into the physical world. This is why painters paint, dancers dance, writers write, and singers sing even if they never get paid or make a living from it. We feel pulled instead of forced to create something. We gravitate toward it. We feel compelled to do it. When we feel like this, we create from a place of abundance instead of lack.

Most of us had goals from inspiration when we were kids. To act on stage. To cook like a chef. To write a book. To explore space. To make art. To save animals. To heal people. To invent something. To make people laugh.

What did you dream of doing when you were a kid?

How would it feel just to do it for fun to any degree you can?

This will reveal to you some of the goals of inspiration you may have forgotten about.

Even as adults, we naturally have goals of inspiration. It could be starting a charity, business, hobby, or animal shelter. It could be raising a family, traveling the world, living off-grid, growing a garden, learning a new language or instrument, running a marathon, or starting a blog.

When we create goals out of inspiration, we are not creating from a place of lack. We don't create because we feel like we *have* to or we need more. We create because we *want* to. This type of creation is an overflowing of love and joy for life. This is the reason why most of us want or have children—not because we want something from them but because we want to share the abundance of what we have with them.

This feeling of deep inspiration comes not from us but through us from something greater than ourselves. I call this feeling divine inspiration, because our ideas of what we want to create seem far bigger than we could have imagined or come up with on our own. It knows no boundaries, limits, or constraints.

It's an expansive force that energizes and lifts us, making us feel "high" on life. In this state, we feel whole, complete, and filled with unconditional love, joy, and peace. It is one of the greatest feelings we can experience.

Everyone has experienced this feeling of pure inspiration. Before moving on, pause and spend a moment recalling a time in your life when you felt an overwhelming desire to create something magnificent because you felt deeply inspired to. It doesn't matter if you actually created it or not; just think of a time when you felt that feeling of inspiration.

Isn't it just one of the most amazing feelings in the entire world? Most of us feel this divine inspiration but then suppress it as soon as we begin thinking about bringing it to life. We begin to think ourselves into doubt, rationalize why we can't achieve these goals, and tell ourselves that they are unrealistic, that we should focus on more important things, and that we're not good enough. As soon as we begin to think about the thought of wanting to create, we completely shut off the source of that inspiration, and we go back to living life in desperation. When we cut off that source, we also cut off feelings of abundance, vitality, ecstasy, joy, and pure unconditional love and go back to feelings of doubt, anxiety, frustration, and sadness.

When we live a life of non-thinking, we don't stop having goals and dreams. We just create goals and dreams out of inspiration instead of desperation.

So how can we tell whether a goal is created out of inspiration or desperation?

Goals created from desperation and inspiration can look very similar from the outside, but they differ greatly under the surface.

A simple way to know if a goal or dream is created out of inspiration is to remember the distinction between thoughts and thinking. Goals and dreams that come in the form of thought are created out of inspiration. Goals and dreams that come from thinking are created out of desperation.

Goals from desperation are typically rooted in fear and make your happiness conditional on achieving them. Goals from inspiration are rooted in love and focus more on the joy of doing over the outcome. The joy comes from the act itself, not just what you externally get out of it. The reason why you create the goal will determine how you will feel while pursuing it.

Goals of inspiration come from identifying what you value and what is most important to you. Is it security? Raising a loving family? Traveling? Creativity? Learning? Peace? Expressing yourself? Goals of inspiration are aligned with your values, while goals of desperation contradict them. For this reason, one person's goal of inspiration can be another person's goal of desperation. It all depends on what your values are.

For an author who values their craft but feels driven by a sense of insecurity, an example of a goal created from desperation would be to want to hit the bestseller list because it would finally make them feel like they were good enough. A goal created from inspiration would be to write a book because they love the act of writing with their whole being.

The first goal was created to try to *prove* they are good at what they do (external validation), and the second was created because they simply *love* what they do. The second aligns with their values, while the first does not.

But for an author who primarily values spreading their message as far as possible, the opposite might be true. For this person, reaching the bestseller list could be a goal of inspiration. It all depends on understanding our own personal value systems.

For most of us, however, goals born from a love of the work itself will lead to greater happiness than goals based on achieving a certain output. And more times than not, falling in love with what you are doing in the present will allow you to achieve many of those external goals you previously had as a byproduct. Love will take you further than sheer effort ever will.

I want to emphasize that I'm not saying we shouldn't have financial goals. There are no right or wrong goals—only goals created from inspiration or desperation. What matters is the source of the goal, not necessarily the goal itself.

For instance, if a person values safety and stability for their family, a goal of making money in order to achieve this could absolutely be a goal of inspiration. But for that same person, making money in order to achieve social status might be a goal of desperation. The key is in asking yourself, What does money give me or allow me to do that I value most?

It's also important to recognize that when you create a goal from inspiration, it does not necessarily mean you are meant to drop everything and devote every moment of your day to it. Most of us are not in a position to do that. But what we can do is *begin* taking small steps toward that goal each day. What matters is not how long you are doing it each day but that you are doing it to some capacity every day.

If your goal of inspiration is to raise the best family you can, what are you doing on a daily basis to help you achieve that goal?

If it is to become the best you can be at your job, what steps are you taking each day to incrementally improve? If it is to grow a garden, can you start with one small herb? If it is to learn a new language, can you learn a word a day?

If it is to travel, what are you doing each day to allow you to do so more often? You may not be able to travel each day, but you can do many things to enable you to travel more often, such as saving a bit more each day, exploring remote work options, or maybe even taking a language class.

There are an infinite number of ways for you to make your goals from inspiration a reality. It's not about *if* you can do it but *how* you can make it happen. Start small and do it at any capacity you can daily. Doing so will create more meaning and fulfillment in your life because you will be making progress on what matters most to you each day. This is how we find more love and joy in the doing and not just the outcome.

So how do we create goals and dreams out of inspiration?

As with surfacing thoughts, creating goals and dreams from divine inspiration isn't something you have to *try* to do. We naturally have thoughts of inspiration all the time. If you look at children, they naturally have the wildest dreams of what they want to do. It almost never registers in their minds that they might not be able to accomplish something. The only difference between us and children is that we have learned to shut down these thoughts of inspiration.

Imagine your inspiration is a river, and thinking is a dam. If a dam is built to block the river, it leads to the death of fish, the disappearance of wildlife, flooding, and the destruction of forests.

Our thinking creates a dam that blocks the river of inspiration within our minds, leading to self-doubt, self-sabotage, and anxiety.

But once the dam is removed, the ecosystem will heal and return to its natural state. The same is true for our minds.

When we're tapped into our intuition and free from the blockages that come from thinking, new inspiring thoughts and ideas can freely come through us as intended, and that is how we "create" goals out of inspiration instead of desperation.

A question that significantly helps me settle my unhelpful thinking and tap into the limitless well of creative possibilities is this:

If I had infinite money, had no fear, and didn't feel the need to receive any recognition, what would I do or create?

Try asking the question and seeing what comes up for you. You'll be surprised at what surfaces when you remove the barriers of fear, criticism, and self-doubt. Let the inspiration rise to the surface, but then don't get caught up in thinking. Allow your true dreams to reveal themselves without shutting them down.

To a mind without the limits of thinking, anything is possible.

if you want to stay alive
nourish your body

if you want to feel alive
nourish your soul

Chapter 10

Nothing Is
Either Good or Bad

*There is nothing either good or bad
but thinking makes it so.*

—WILLIAM SHAKESPEARE

Picture a piano with eighty-eight keys. When we look at a piano, we don't point out specific keys and say that they are "bad" or "wrong." We only think a particular key is "wrong" if it sounds unpleasant in the context of a piece of music. Outside of the context of a song, the piano has no wrong keys. Only notes that can be combined in infinite ways.

Just like how there are no wrong keys on the piano, there are no "wrong" decisions in life. Only different paths. All we have to do is choose which to take. If we categorize paths as right or wrong, we close ourselves off from the ocean of opportunities available to us.

Now, when I say there is no right or wrong, I don't mean that this is a license to cause harm; it is absolutely not. What I mean is that there is not one correct path when navigating our personal decisions on this journey of life. Knowing there is no right or wrong relieves us of the pressure to choose the "right" one.

Take, for example, a hike up a mountain. On this hike, there will be different spots where you can stop to look at the view. There are no "wrong" spots to stop to take in the magnificence of nature, and by being open to all places, we can see the view from different vantage points we haven't seen before. If you judge an option too soon, you may be missing out on the most beautiful view yet. Even an option that seems lesser may hold unexpected benefits if you explore it further.

Instead of looking for right or wrong, good or bad, look for truth without judgment.

But beware of falsehoods that you may have convinced yourself are the truth. The truth is rarely in the extremes but somewhere in between. The actual truth is not subjective. If it is "true" for one person but not for another, then it is not a universal truth. Look for what is universally true for every conscious human being on the planet, no matter who they are, where they're from, and what their background may be. That is the truth and where you'll find everything you've been searching for. Remember that the truth is only ever inside, so don't try to look for it outside of you.

What you obtain externally can always be lost, but what you find within yourself can never be taken away.

an intelligent person is constantly learning
a wise person is always unlearning

Chapter 11

How to Follow Your Intuition

Have the courage to follow your heart and intuition.
They somehow already know what you truly
want to become. Everything else is secondary.

—STEVE JOBS

Although there are no right or wrong decisions we can make, just like there are no right or wrong keys on a piano, there are decisions that are more aligned with us than others depending on the context.

So then how do we choose which path to take? When we make decisions, we want to rely on non-thinking. The more we try to think, analyze, and ask for outside opinions, the more it causes unnecessary anxiety and frustration. Most of the time, we already know deep down what to do. This is often referred to as your intuition, gut feeling, or inner wisdom. When we seek outside counsel, we're actually just looking to confirm what our intuition is already telling us. But inviting an outside opinion will more than likely lead to more self-doubt.

Only you can know what is right for you. No one else can tell you this. There will be mentors and teachers who can offer guidance, but the best ones will tell you to listen to your intuition and look within yourself for the answer. The truth is only ever within you. This is why many of us experience regret after following another's advice. Deep down, we know we shouldn't have ignored our instincts.

Your intuition will always lead you to where you need to go. It is a real-time inner navigation system that will tell you when to take a detour and which path to follow if you encounter a roadblock. It will guide you to exactly where you need to go, but the path it takes may surprise you. Do not doubt yourself. Trust that your intuition is bringing you exactly where you need to be.

So what does following your intuition look like?

When you're following your intuition, you're tapped into something greater than yourself. You're in a state of non-thinking and in direct connection with the Universe. Intuition is not a form of thinking. It's a sense of *knowing*. You're not *thinking* about what to do; you just *know* what to do. It's not about making the "right" choice but about trusting yourself and understanding you are choosing what is best for your current situation.

Instead of trying to make a decision based on whether something is right or wrong, good or bad, make it based on the decision that feels most expansive and aligned with who you are and what you value most. Your intuition will tell you what that choice is when you ask.

When you follow your intuition, you are guided by an innate intelligence we all have, and you will always know what you need to do. To return to a concept from a previous chapter, trusting your intuition is how you operate when you're in a flow state. When you're in this zone, tasks seem effortless, and you open yourself up to information and opportunities beyond your logical mind.

Intuition is how mothers know how to take care of their newborns without having much or any training. It's how you know your friend may not be fine even though they say they are.

You likely use intuition more often than you're aware of. When considering intuition, many automatically assume it's only used within creative tasks and projects, but it is also highly useful in navigating life whenever there may not be one obvious "right" answer. It is that gut feeling that tells us to leave or start a relationship or job or to move to a new place. It tells us when to marry someone or start a family, what new thing we should try or which old habit we should stop, and whether to talk to a stranger who might end up becoming a close friend. It is that still, quiet voice that always nudges us toward the things we need and the things that will help us grow most in the moment. Fear keeps us where we are. Intuition leads us to who we want to be.

This does not mean we should not use our intellect, logic, and reason. Rather, it is about using them without negative judgment and trusting our intuitive decisions so that we don't end up in a spiral of overthinking and suffering. The key is to use our thoughts instead of thinking.

For example, if we are cooking with a recipe or brainstorming new ideas for work, we want to use our thoughts to help guide us. This means neutrally observing the situation and responding accordingly but without attaching judgment to it. Too often, our thinking will kick in when executing these actions, and we'll end up thinking, "I'm not a good cook" or "I never have any good ideas." This negative story we create around the task is unnecessary and unhelpful.

Our thinking minds will convince us that we must have everything figured out. But buying into this belief will only cause additional stress and suffering. We don't have to have it all figured out, nor can we. How can our limited minds possibly understand and try to manipulate the entire world to our desires?

The great news is that we don't have to know everything. All we have to do is trust in our intuition and have faith that our inner wisdom will show us the best way forward. When you ask people who are the most abundant, joyful, and successful how they made it and what led them to make the decisions they did, if you keep digging and asking why, they will eventually reveal that they followed their intuition. If they had listened only to logic and reason, they would never have taken a leap of faith to pursue their dreams.

Our intuition can see things the mind cannot. Most of the greatest achievements and creations of our time were once deemed impossible and therefore irrational to attempt. But we do not live in a world of impossibility. We live in a world of infinite possibilities. Following our hearts can be risky, but we guarantee our unhappiness when we do not.

Your intuition is usually the choice that makes you feel a tinge of fear because it requires you to step into the unknown to create a new reality rather than stay in your familiar one. Nothing that grows can stay the same—especially you.

Diving in headfirst to explore the unknown is something humans were created to do and cannot resist. The unknown is where we feel most alive. Although our minds crave certainty, our hearts desire freedom. We live in an illusion of certainty. Most of what we have can be lost or taken away at a moment's notice. We all know the only constant is change, yet we spend most of our energy trying to fight what is natural and inevitable and wonder why we are suffering so much. It is not change that we should fear but staying the same.

Most things in life are out of our control. This is not to say that we should give up because we can't control our lives; it's quite the opposite. The path to peace is not to pursue certainty but to relax into uncertainty. To surrender to the ebbs and flows of life and accept things as they are instead of how you think they should be. It's not about trying to force things to happen a certain way but about trusting that you will *be* okay no matter what happens.

While we can't control everything that happens, we can always control our reactions and therefore our emotions. This is how we can choose to be happy—by choosing to let go of our thinking. Isn't that what ultimately matters at the end of the day? It's not what we have but how we feel inside that is the true measure of success, joy, and fulfillment.

We have the gift of imagination, which means our creative potential is limitless, but we create stress for ourselves when we think we need to figure out "the how" to make it happen. At this point, most people give up or continue down the path of brute force to try to bring it to life and suffer daily for it. We tell ourselves we must suffer for what we want, but that is not true if we trust our intuition instead. Our job is determining *what* we want, not necessarily how to get it. The *how* is up to the Universe, and delegating this responsibility is ideal because there are an infinite number of ways to bring about what we want in life.

Our intuition will rarely show us every detail of how we can create what we imagine, but it will always show us the very next step to take in the present moment. Trying to figure it all out in advance will only lead to overthinking. The path forward is only revealed when we begin walking.

We can always get what we desire in life; it just may happen in a different way or at a different time from *how* or *when* we expect it to happen.

Our intuition speaks to us all the time. You know that small voice inside that somehow constantly *knows* what you should do? It's that gut feeling you get when you know what you need to do. Have you ever regretted not following that feeling? Have you ever felt compelled to do something for no logical reason, but then amazing things happened when you followed it?

That is your intuition.

Our intuition speaks to us through thoughts and feelings. But remember that there's a stark difference between thoughts and thinking. Thinking is the negative judgment of our intuition, the worry that blocks us from following our hearts.

Your intuition is the choice that feels most expansive, aligned, and unknown. It is always calm, clear, direct, and unattached.

It will often go against your logical, rational mind, so be prepared. It will tell you to grow, be more creative, and try new things. It will softly beckon you to pursue what you truly want instead of following what everyone else says you should want. When you follow your intuition, you create a life of freedom, love, and joy.

So why don't more people listen to their intuition? Because of fear.

Listening to our intuition can be daunting. This is because our intuition lives in the realm of the unknown. We fear the unknown because it's unpredictable. But it's only when we step into the unknown that we can begin opening ourselves up to opportunities to create a different experience of life than the one we are living.

Other people may not agree with your decisions, but you are not here to sacrifice your peace for other peoples' preferences. You are here to learn, grow, and love—and many times, doing what will help you grow the most will make others around you uncomfortable because they are not ready for it. And that is okay, because everyone grows on their own time. But you don't have to let other people's fears become your reality. Don't let them stop you from doing what makes you feel alive and inspired.

Henry Ford once said, "Whether you *think* you can or can't, you're right." If we live our lives thinking we can't, we block ourselves from all the possibilities of what we can do. The first step is realizing that we already know what to do. The only thing holding us back is fear. When we release the brake in our mind and realize that it's just our thinking holding us back, we return to our natural state of abundance, creativity, and pure possibility. Surrender, trust your intuition, take the next step in front of you, and let the Universe do the rest.

are you making decisions
to feel safe
or to feel *free*?

Chapter 12

Creating Space for Insight

Today I make space for miracles. I recognize that it's not how big a miracle is that's important, but how much room I create for it.

—KYLE GRAY

The Story of the Zen Master and a Scholar: Empty Your Cup

Once upon a time, there was a wise Zen master. People traveled from far away to seek his help. In return, he would teach them and show them the way to enlightenment. One day, a scholar visited the master for advice. "I have come to ask you to teach me about Zen," the scholar said.

Soon, it became obvious that the scholar was already full of his own opinions and knowledge about Zen. He interrupted the master repeatedly with his own stories and failed to listen to what the master had to say. The master calmly suggested that they should have tea.

Once they had been seated, the master gently poured his guest a cup. The cup was filled, yet he kept pouring until the cup overflowed onto the table, onto the floor, and finally onto the scholar's robes. The scholar cried, "Stop! The cup is full already. Can't you see?"

"Exactly," the Zen master replied with a smile. "You are like this cup—so full of ideas that nothing more will fit in. Come back to me with an empty cup."

*   *   *

It is ironic how much could be written about nothing. That's what space is: nothing. When we study the universe, we realize that everything comes from nothing. For there to be creation, there must first be space.

This is equally true for our minds. If you want something new to be created, such as new thoughts, you must first create space to receive these ideas. Like the teacup, if your mind is full of old thinking, you won't have space for new thoughts. And new thoughts are necessary if you want to create the change you seek.

This is the flip side of using your intuition. While it is important to trust our instincts, we also want to make sure that we don't close ourselves off to new ideas, perspectives, and information. If you sense yourself feeling afraid when encountering a new idea, let that be an indicator that this is a moment to dig deep and examine that fear. On the other side of that fear may be a whole world of possibility that contains what you are looking for, if you remain open to it.

The goal is to find a balance so that we do not doubt ourselves but also can walk through the world with an open mind. By challenging long-held beliefs and letting go of what no longer serves us, we create room for new ideas that can enrich our lives.

The way we can create this space is through non-thinking. When we stop our strenuous mental efforts and quiet our minds, we create space for new thoughts and ideas to enter. Judgment closes the mind, while questions open it. Continually asking questions that challenge our current thinking is one of the best ways to create space in our minds.

All the magic happens in this space of nothingness. For instance, all athletes go through intense training periods, but the best athletes know that they need an equally intense period of rest afterward to stay in peak performance. It is during this rest period that they recover, build muscle, and become stronger. The space they create through rest is where the progress they want from the workout manifests.

We've all experienced moments where we have created space for thoughts of inspiration and had ideas spontaneously pop into our minds. You may have experienced a time when you were struggling with a certain situation or decision in your life and couldn't figure it out, but all of a sudden the solution flashed into your mind while you were showering, walking, or doing something relatively relaxing. Those are moments when we tend to create space psychologically and thus are more open and available for ideas to come.

Friedrich Nietzsche, one of the great German philosophers of the nineteenth century who revolutionized the way we view morality and religion, had a routine practice for creating space to aid him in generating ideas. He would go on extensive walks in the middle of writing his books and would bring a small notepad with him to jot down ideas he thought of during his stroll. It is documented that Nietzsche thought out and wrote the majority of his book *The Wanderer and His Shadow* during those daily walks.

Albert Einstein was a scientific genius who similarly knew the importance of this concept. When Einstein was stuck on a difficult problem, he would stop working on it and play the violin instead. As he played, the answer would spontaneously come to him not from force but from calming the mind and creating space for inspiration to flow.

We don't have to work tirelessly to figure everything out. Even the people we deem geniuses knew that effort wouldn't always produce their greatest discoveries. Just like how rest is required for us to perform our best, space is required to help us discover the best ideas.

Many times, the answer we are looking for is where we least expect it and can only be found when

we take a step back to create space for a new perspective. With the correct understanding and space,
we can also receive insights about any challenge we
may face.

We're only ever one thought, one insight, and
one idea away from living an entirely different experience of life.

what we do not question
controls us

what we question
frees us

Chapter 13

Potential Obstacles When Living in Non-thinking

*Don't think. It complicates things. Just feel, and
if it feels like home, then follow its path.*

—R. M. DRAKE

If you've been applying the principles in this book,
I hope you've been able to find moments of non-
thinking and experience the peace that they bring.
If not, do not be disheartened; it will come with
practice. As you continue your journey with non-
thinking, you may encounter some roadblocks.

**Don't worry; this is a normal part of the awak-
ening process.** And you've already learned the most
challenging part: to practice non-thinking and prevent
negative thinking from controlling your life.

But we can also work to anticipate and solve problems ahead of time so that it's less daunting if you experience them. Let's explore a few questions you may
have as you continue on your journey of non-thinking.

Will Practicing Non-thinking
Make Me Less Productive?

Once you have been able to experience peace, you might begin to worry that you're not as productive now, have lost your "edge," or are lazier. But this couldn't be further from the truth. The reality is that we are most productive when we are working in a state of non-thinking. We are more effective, have better ideas, experience less resistance and stress, and don't procrastinate as much when we're not thinking.

You may find yourself working less because less time is spent on anxiety and worry. Or perhaps you finally see that rest is equally important to work, and you begin giving your body what it needs rather than ignoring it. You have begun to see how slowing down gives you a sense of peace and joy that is hard to experience while overworking and frantically trying to accomplish the next task. Things that used to cause stress no longer make you feel as anxious.

If you have been living in a state of fight or flight for a while, you may have become so used to the feeling of anxiety that it feels "normal." Living your life without as many of those feelings will understandably feel different and strange. This is all normal and is simply a growing pain that will dissipate with time. As you continue to live your life in non-thinking, peace will become your new normal.

Does Practicing Non-thinking Mean Avoiding Reality?

A common misconception is that practicing non-thinking means avoiding and ignoring reality or that it means walking through life with your blinders on. But it is the exact opposite. Living life through non-thinking is accepting reality as it is instead of what we *think* it should be. The practice of non-thinking is about being deeply present and holding a space of non-judgment for everything that is happening in the world around us and within our minds. Through non-thinking, we can finally confront everything we are afraid of and no longer let those fears control us. Non-thinking is how we can let go of everything that isn't reality to find peace.

How Can I Work or Solve Problems without Thinking?

The same principle of non-thinking applies to work as it does to navigating life. In the case of work or solving problems, we want to utilize thoughts instead of thinking.

When working, much of what we do is solving problems that require solutions that do not exist yet, which can only come from thoughts. When we think, we shut down ideas and criticize them, the situation, or even ourselves, creating counterproductive and unnecessary stress. In fact, we are significantly *less* effective and creative when we are in a fight-or-flight state. This type of thinking has no benefit to us or the work we produce and rarely creates the outcome and emotions we want to experience.

The following are examples of thinking during work:

This is going to be so difficult.

It's going to take so much time.

I hate projects like this.

Why does this always happen to me?

I can't do this.

I'm not good enough to do this.

This is terrible.

I'm going to fail.

The following are examples of thoughts during work:

Is there a better way to do this?

Who can I ask for help?

What if we tried it this way?

What would happen if . . . ?

(insert any idea, insight, or breakthrough)

You may also refer to the "Thoughts versus Thinking" chart in chapter 4 (and in the Resources section in the back of the book) to help you distinguish between the two in the context of work.

What If I Begin to Feel Anxiety, Worry, and Doubt Creeping Back In?

A reason that we may feel anxiety, worry, and doubt once we experience peace is that thinking all the time uses a colossal amount of time and energy. Most of us are used to spending the majority of our day in a state of stress (thinking). When we stop thinking, the energy we used to spend thinking is now "freed up," but it hasn't been directed anywhere yet, so we tend to return to our old patterns of funneling that energy back into thinking, because that is how we were conditioned and what feels familiar. What we can do instead is channel the newfound energy into our goals of inspiration.

What tends to help many people in this stage is to have an "activation ritual." An activation ritual is a morning routine that helps them get into a state of non-thinking and flow. It can be any activity or routine that helps you feel grounded and allows you to practice getting into a state of non-thinking. Examples might be exercising, meditating, performing breathwork, praying, journaling, or making tea. It does not matter what the activity is as long as it helps you feel centered. An activation ritual enables you to build momentum in a positive direction immediately when you wake up so that it's easier to stay in that state of non-thinking for the rest of the day. An object in motion will stay in motion. I never understood why spiritual masters have morning routines until I understood the power of momentum and grounding to aid non-thinking.

If you begin to feel like something's wrong because you feel way too peaceful and content, know that it's only your mind trying to make you think again. Your mind is the greatest salesperson and knows exactly what to say to lure you back into its vicious cycle of destructive thinking. It is in this moment that you have the choice to have faith in the unknown and stay in the feeling of happiness, peace, and love or to go back to the old patterns of familiar pain and psychological suffering. We can either choose to be free and happy in the unknown or choose to be confined and suffer in the familiar.

If you do fall back into thinking, it is completely okay. Do not beat yourself up about it. Don't feel guilty that it happened. Punishing yourself is unhelpful because it will only exacerbate your thinking. Know that it is human to think. When you catch yourself thinking, simply follow the PAUSE method (in chapter 7 or in the Resources section at the back of the book) and gently remind yourself that you have the ability to return yourself to a state of peace, happiness, and love at any time. Be compassionate with yourself as this process repeats; the transition can happen painlessly and effortlessly if you let it.

to the person who is at peace
with the feeling of fear
the whole Universe yields

Chapter 14

Unconditional Love

The greatest power that mankind could ever achieve is the power of unconditional love. This is when people love with no limitations, conditions, or boundaries.

—TONY GREEN

I learned unconditional love from my extraordinary partner, Makenna. For most of my life, I always questioned everything. I had to know the reason why things were the way they were. I couldn't just experience life without knowing the meaning and reasoning behind everything.

Naturally, as anyone in a relationship would, after about a year, I asked Makenna why she loved me. She replied that she didn't know why; she just knew she did. Then she asked me why I loved her, and I listed dozens of different reasons why. It ranged from her beautiful smile to her adorable laugh, how pure her heart is, how much she loves her family, and how intelligent she is. The list went on almost indefinitely.

We dated for seven years before we got married, and every few months after that first time I asked, I would ask her again why she loved me. And to this day, she always answers the same way: "I don't know; I just know that I love you—a lot."

This answer bothered me for a long time. I didn't understand how she could possibly not know why she loved me. I could list a thousand reasons why I loved her, but she couldn't list even one. But I loved her so much that I accepted it and continued loving her anyway.

But then one day, I decided to ask myself a different question, and it led to an epiphany that changed my life forever.

Instead of asking myself why Makenna couldn't list any reasons why she loved me, I asked myself, Do I love her because of her laugh or because she loves helping others? What happens if she doesn't laugh one day or doesn't help someone that day? Do I stop loving her if she doesn't do the things I said I loved about her?

I realized that if I create reasons for why I love her, then it makes my love for her conditional on those specific traits or actions, as if I would stop loving her if she doesn't do them. This, of course, is not true.

At that moment, I finally realized that Makenna couldn't list reasons why she loved me because her love for me was unconditional. While there are things she loves about me, there are no reasons *why* she loves me. If she had reasons, it would mean she only loved me if I were exemplifying those traits.

Her love for me is not based on my mood or what I do; her love for me goes beyond all "reasons" and does not come from a place of reciprocity. She does not love me because I love her, nor is she loving me because of what I can do for her. She experiences an abundance of love that she gifts me unconditionally.

I learned to make my love for Makenna unconditional by not placing reasons or conditions on it. There is simply an outpouring of an overwhelming and indescribable appreciation for her, and I can't help but love her no matter what. This type of love comes not from external reasons but from within. It is the infinite source we all came from.

We are all connected to this pure, unconditional love, which is the Universe, God, or whichever name you choose to use. The only thing that prevents this connection is our own thinking, which creates an illusion of separation from that unconditional love.

When we let go of needing reasons to love one another, there is no end to how much love we can discover.

courage is not the absence of fear
but the presence of love
in the midst of fear

Chapter 15

Now What?

There will come a time when you believe everything is finished; that will be the beginning.

—LOUIS L'AMOUR

Although this is the end of the book, it is just the beginning of a new life for you. You are only ever one thought away from peace, love, and joy. Remember this and keep it close to your heart, because it is all the hope you need when life becomes difficult. In the beginning, I promised you that you would not be the same person you were before reading this book. If you began reading this book with the intention of having an open and willing mind, then you most likely have had insights that changed the way you think, and thus you are not the same person as you were before.

Once you see something new from an insight, you cannot unsee it. Once your consciousness expands, it cannot contract again. We may forget from time to time and experience the suffering caused by think-ing. But as soon as we become aware of this, we can find love, peace, and joy in the present.

If this seems too simple, it is just your mind caus-ing you to think again. The truth is simple and always will be. The truth is not something you think but something you know and feel deep in your soul. Lis-ten to that still inner wisdom inside you that knows all of this. Let it guide you through your life.

We are most fulfilled when we listen to our souls. The world will tell us that we are not enough, that we are missing something, that we don't have every-thing we want. People will bombard us with their opinions, judgments, and advice. Know that they are innocently caught up in their thinking. They may be coming from a place of good intention, but you are not obligated to listen to them.

Everything you could ever want or need is already inside of you. You are already all the love, joy, peace, and fulfillment that you seek. It is only when we for-get this fact and get caught up in our thinking that we do not see it.

Continue to live in this state of serenity and let go of what does not serve you. Follow your intuition and what feels expansive, aligned, and unknown. The more you do this, the more abundance you will create in your life. You are now equipped with everything you need to know about how to stop your own psy-chological suffering and access a state of peace, love, and joy, which is always available to you. Perhaps you have already experienced the bliss of knowing and embodying this.

It is no coincidence that you have picked up this book and that we have been able to share our journey here together. It is truly humbling and an incredible gift that you have allowed me to guide you through this infinitely beautiful experience we call life. Keep sharing your love and light with the world.

From My Heart to Yours,

Joseph

transformation is not a result to be achieved
but a byproduct of letting go
    to be *experienced*

What Should You Read Next?

Thank you from the bottom of my heart for taking the time to read this book. If you enjoyed *Don't Believe Everything You Think*, you may be interested in my other writing as well.

Every week, I share a new piece of writing through my "Nuggets of Wisdom" newsletter, which contains one simple, perspective-shifting idea to expand your mind and help you find more peace, joy, and abundance.

Subscribers are also the first to hear about my newest books and projects.

Join our community of seekers and sign up for my newsletter at

josephnguyen.org/newsletter

Or you may sign up by scanning the QR code below:

Looking for More Relief from Overthinking?

My next book, *The Overthinker's Guide to Making Decisions*, **available November 2025**, is a guide for transforming paralyzing overthinking into clear, intuitive decision making.

As a companion to *Don't Believe Everything You Think*, this book invites you to move beyond intellectual understanding and into practical application—with essays, guided exercises, and journaling prompts to help you frame decisions, identify hidden fears, and uncover the root cause of what's keeping you stuck—so your next decision comes not from fear but from freedom.

PRACTICE

This section contains guides designed to help you implement non-thinking into your daily life. The guides are split into two themes—Inner Work and Outer Work—to help you integrate non-thinking into both your inner world and your approach to the world around you.

While letting go of overthinking is a simple concept, it is by no means easy to put into practice. If you are struggling with it, it is okay. Most of us have been stuck in our own thinking for decades and have never tried to stop. It will understandably be different and difficult. There is no need to beat yourself up for not being immediately "good" at something new. Give yourself compassion and space to experiment as we do with children when they are learning something for the first time. The more you practice, the better you will get. Trust that it will come with time. The fact that you are here means you are already well on your path to peace, and it is inevitable if you stay the course.

Inner Work

The following guides focus on the inner workings of your mind. They lead you through practical steps to combat overthinking and instead implement non-thinking to help you find more peace throughout your day.

the absence of thinking (self)
is the presence of peace (divine)

How to Let Go of
Negative Thinking: PAUSE

To help you remember the five-step process for letting go of your thinking, use the acronym PAUSE. Whenever you're feeling overwhelmed by your thinking, *pause* and remember that you have the power to let go of it at any time.

P—Pause and take deep breaths to calm your nervous system and ground yourself in the present. Become aware that you are thinking, but do not judge it.

A—Ask yourself, "Is this thinking making me feel the way I want?" or "Do I want to keep suffering?" If not, you always have the choice to let your thinking go in order to find peace.

U—Understand that you have the choice to stop and let go of it.

S—Say and repeat the mantra "Thinking is the root cause of suffering" to help quiet the mind from thinking until it subsides and passes.

E—Experience your emotions fully without judgment, resistance, or thinking (don't think; just feel).

Repeat this process until you have calmed your nervous system and the thinking has passed.

Potential Obstacles and Solutions

As you are working on letting go of your thinking, you may run into some potential obstacles that make it difficult. Here are some common things that will keep you in a state of anxiety and fear as well as the solutions.

* * *

Not Wanting to Let Go

Sometimes you may not want to let go because you believe it's what got you to where you are. While this is partially true, it's important to recognize that what got you here won't get you there. If you want to break the vicious cycle of suffering and the same self-destructive patterns repeating in your life, you'll have to do something different.

Insanity is doing the same thing over and over again but expecting a different result. The real question is, Do you want to be at peace or not? If you remember that thinking is the root cause of all of your suffering and decide that you do not want to be unhappy any longer, then you will be able to make the leap of faith into non-thinking.

Lack of Faith

It is difficult to believe that we can change our lives for the better, and it requires a big leap of faith to make that change by trusting ourselves in a different way than we have before. But for there to even be a possibility that your life could be a life filled with joy, peace, and love every day, you must first believe that it is possible.

You are part of something much bigger: the life force that has been taking care of and guiding you this whole time (Universe/God/Intuition). Having faith in our intuition without being able to fully comprehend it with our finite minds is difficult and even scary, but it is how we can experience total peace in our lives instead of worrying about and trying to control everything.

Fear

It is perfectly normal to feel fear when trusting the unknown. In fact, it would be strange not to! Fear is an indication that something is important to us, so this is a sign that your mind is trying to protect you.

Everything we want is on the other side of fear. The way out is by going deep within yourself to see and know that you will be okay no matter what. You might not be able to eliminate the fear, but you can recognize that this fear cannot and will not kill you. Yet if you listen to it, it will take the life of your dreams instead. Fear is only an emotion, one that you are more than strong enough to hold space for. The way out of fear is by breathing through it and following the PAUSE framework. Thinking is the root cause of fear. If you don't think, there is no fear.

A Guide to Neutralizing Fear

The only thing stopping us from doing what we truly desire in this world and following our intuition is fear, which is created from our thinking. This is why thinking is the root cause of all psychological and emotional suffering.

Although our fear will tell us that we are afraid of external things, such as a negative event, really what we fear is how we imagine we'll feel if an undesired outcome happens. Fear is internal, not external. This is great news because we can always change and let go of what is internal.

To overcome fear, you must question what it is you are truly afraid of and then see the truth behind this fear—that it is an illusion designed to keep us in our comfort zones and nothing more. It is only when we see what is actually happening in our minds that we can let go of it to be free.

Most of the time, when we feel fear, we try to suppress or avoid it, which only ends up magnifying the fear and giving it more power.

When we have the courage to accept and examine our fears and look at the truth beyond our thinking, the illusion of the fear dissolves, and we fall back into peace. In this state of non-thinking, a state of pure presence and complete peace, we always know what to do and may move toward it, even if the fear lingers. In this state, fear cannot hold us back any longer.

When you are feeling afraid, use the following guide to neutralize the fear and work through it. If you do this, all of your greatest desires await you on the other side.

*   *   *

Define the Fear
What are you afraid of? Be specific.

Inquire and Examine
What's behind Your Thinking
Take a closer look at the fear. Remember that what you're truly afraid of is not what you think will happen but how you think it will make you feel if it happens. What are you afraid of feeling?

1. If what you're afraid of happens, what are you worried it will mean about you? What conclusions have you drawn about yourself? Example: If (insert what you're afraid of doing or what might happen), then it means I'm (insert conclusion).

2. Is this conclusion valid? Or is it a story you've been telling yourself?

3. How does this conclusion (thinking) make you feel?

4. What is it costing you to continue believing this thinking? Write down as much as you can with specificity and really feel it. Be as detailed as possible.

5. Can you see how this thinking creates a condition that causes you suffering?

6. Are you ready to stop believing in this thinking and let go of it?

7. How does it feel when you imagine letting it go?

8. What is your intuition telling you right now?

9. How does your intuition feel in comparison to your thinking?

Set an intention to continue following your intuition, and remember that you can repeat this exercise any time you need it.

A Guide to Non-thinking Decision-Making

One of the most difficult parts of adopting non-thinking is learning to make decisions by listening to and trusting our intuition instead of falling back into our old patterns of overthinking and ruminating. Use the following guide to help you create a new behavior for yourself.

* * *

Define the Decision

Write down the decision you are trying to make as simply as you can.

Inquire and Let Go by Asking Yourself These Questions

1. What are you afraid will happen if you make this decision?

2. If you dig deeper, what are you actually afraid of? What is the feeling you fear?

3. What story is this fear telling you? Write out exactly what it is saying in great detail without filtering anything. Do you have evidence that this story is true? Or might it be just a story?

4. What's the cost of listening to this thinking and fear? What is it costing you personally, physically, mentally, emotionally, and spiritually? List as much as you can.

5. Can you see how much suffering this thinking is causing you? Are you ready to let go of it now?

6. If you let go of all external opinions, advice, and influences, what do you intuitively know you want to do? What decision feels most expansive and aligned with you?

7. How would it feel to follow your intuition?

8. Write down what your intuition is telling you and what it is inviting you to do right now.

9. Can you see how following your intuition will help you feel the way you want and create the life you desire?

If you are ready, make the commitment now to follow your intuition even if you feel fear. You are greater than your fears and stronger than you think. Let go and trust you will be okay and that things will work out for you.

A Guide to Overcoming Destructive Habits

As you create more space and learn to let go of your thinking, you may become aware of a lot of negative, destructive habits that are making you more prone to suffering. The following guide can help you break these destructive habits.

*   *   *

Become aware of the behavior you want to change and confirm that you genuinely want to alter it. Understand that if you want to stop the vicious cycle of suffering, you will have to change and let go of the beliefs you're holding onto that are creating the suffering. If you don't want to change it, there's no point in continuing forward. If you do want to change it, let's begin the process of letting go.

Write down in exact, meticulous detail what happens with this behavior (what it is, how many times it happens, when it happens, etc.). Don't spare any details.

1. What are you feeling in the moment right before you begin the behavior? What's the feeling that triggers the behavior? Be honest with yourself.

2. What specific thinking patterns are going on? What are you saying to yourself in the moment when this happens? Describe it in exact detail.

3. What beliefs do you have about this habit? What conclusions have you made that compel

you to feel like you have to perform this behavior/action?

4. How do you feel when you believe that thinking?

5. What do you believe will happen if you don't perform the behavior? In other words, what do you believe the consequences will be if you don't perform the action?

6. Is it absolutely true that these things will happen if you don't perform the behavior?

7. Can you see how destructive this thinking is and how much it causes you to suffer?

8. Are you willing to let this thinking and behavior go now?

A Guide to Creating Momentum in Your Day

How you start your day will create momentum for how the rest of your day will go. For instance, if you start your day with behaviors that trigger anxiety (perhaps for you that is checking your phone or answering emails), you'll be starting your day in a stressful, fight-or-flight mode of thinking, which will make it more difficult to find peace in the rest of your day. Creating an activation ritual or morning routine can help you enter a state of non-thinking and enable you to align with your highest self. This is why all the greatest spiritual masters have morning rituals or routines.

To start planning out your ideal morning routine, make a list of the things that help you create a state of non-thinking. Consider behaviors as well as environmental stimuli.

Then pick only one or two items on the list and try practicing them every morning for a week. Start small and don't overwhelm yourself.

After a week, evaluate your morning routine. How is it making you feel? Is it taking the right amount of time? Are you finding all the elements beneficial? Do you feel that you want to add or swap out any items on the list? If so, only make one change at a time, remembering that too much change too fast can be counterproductive to your goal and more difficult to sustain in the long term. Try your new routine for another week and then reflect again.

Repeat this process until you have a morning routine that supports you on your path to non-thinking.

Outer Work

The first set of guides were created to help you end suffering and support you in mastering your inner world to find peace within. Now it is time to consider how you're interacting with the world around you as you seek to stay aligned with your true self on the path to peace.

gratitude is acceptance of what is
   hope is understanding nothing lasts forever
      peace is being unattached to what is in
            the mind

Designing a Non-thinking Environment

Your environment either will induce and support the state of non-thinking or can make you more prone to thinking.

Although we create our reality from the inside out, our environment has a large impact on us, so it is important to create an environment that is conducive to non-thinking. Creating a calm space and limiting distractions can make it easier to let go of thinking, which means that you won't have to expend as much effort to get yourself in that zone.

Similarly, if you eliminate many of the things that you know can trigger you to go back into thinking, then it will be easier to stay in a peaceful state of non-thinking for longer. Remember that changing your environment and not yourself will not work long term. But changing your environment can be a crucial support as you work on the important changes within. A delicate blend of both will be what you need to create a beautiful life you love.

Creating a Non-thinking Environment

Use your intuition and ask yourself this question:

> What would be the most impactful things I could do right now to help myself get into and maintain a peaceful, non-thinking state throughout my day?

Write down any and all ideas that come to mind, and don't filter anything—big ideas and little ones,

ones you've tried before and ones you haven't. Maybe you have different ideas for different environments, such as home and work. Allow your intuition to speak to you and tune into what feels most aligned with you.

After writing down all of your ideas, look over your list. Select the one idea that would have the biggest impact on your life and try to implement it this week. Then try implementing the next most impactful idea once you've begun seeing the benefits of the first. Working like this, make your way down the list until you've tried everything. Start small and don't try to make too many changes at once, as too much change can be hard to sustain.

It helps to journal as you go about your experiences. What was helpful? What wasn't? How did trying these ideas impact your experiences? This way, you'll have a record of your experiences and can fine-tune your system going forward.

Removing Thinking Triggers

Step 1: List the things that make you more likely to start overthinking, ruminating, and becoming anxious. Consider ideas in each of the following categories:

Physical Health
The things that impact your body and can make you more prone to experiencing anxiety and overthinking.

Examples: Foods, stimulants, alcohol, dehydration, lack of sleep, not moving your body, and so on.

Physical Environment
The things in your physical environment that can make you more prone to experiencing anxiety and overthinking. Examples: Noise, temperature, location, music, meditation, and so on.

Digital Environment
The things on your phone, computer, or TV that can make you more prone to experiencing anxiety and overthinking. Examples: Checking your phone, notifications, email, and so on.

Digital Consumption
The media/content that can make you more prone to experiencing anxiety and overthinking. Examples: social media, news notifications, and so on.

Step 2: Reorganize and rank your thinking triggers.
After filling out each category, organize and identify the top three triggers that affect you the most within each category. Put a number from 1 to 3 beside each of those triggers, with 1 being the one that affects you the most.

Step 3: Identify and implement ideas.
For each of those top triggers, use your intuition to come up with ways to remove or greatly minimize the trigger and write it down. Then choose the one

idea that would have the greatest impact and try to eliminate it this week. Next, choose one to try the week after. Continue this way until you've experimented with removing each of the triggers you listed. Remember that if you try an idea and it doesn't successfully remove the trigger, you may need to come up with a new idea for this trigger.

Step 4: Journal your insights and discoveries.
Write down the insights you have while going through this specific exercise. What seems to be working for you, and what doesn't? Which triggers are easy to remove, and which are difficult? Do you need to try a different strategy for removing a trigger? What did you become aware of while going through this exercise? What surprised you? What patterns did you notice? What does it cost you to continue to have these triggers in your life? What would happen if you removed them? What intentions would you like to set?

Creating Goals of Inspiration

The source of our goals determines how we feel while pursuing them. Goals from desperation breed anxiety, urgency, and stress, while goals from inspiration feel expansive, aligned, and exciting.

The key is to create goals that align with what we value most instead of just striving for external outcomes or validation.

* * *

Here are some questions to help you create your goal from inspiration:

- If you had infinite resources and never had to work again, what would you do with your time?

- What do you value most in life? What goals can you create that help you express those values daily?

- What have you always wanted to do but haven't had time or are afraid to do?

- What activities feel most expansive and aligned with you?

- What are some of your favorite ways to express your creativity?

- What have you dreamed about doing since you were a little kid?

Look at the answers to these questions and use them as inspiration to create a goal that allows you to express and embody what you value most. They should be focused on falling in love with the activity you are doing rather than just the outcome of it. It doesn't matter how long you perform this activity each day. The important thing is that you are working on it to any small degree you can, and eventually, you'll carve out more time as you go on. When you make time for what you love, it naturally grows, and so will your love for life itself.

The inspiring goal does not have to be grandiose. It can be small and simple. Size is irrelevant. All that matters is how the goal makes you feel.

Avoid making a goal *solely* around money. A monetary goal is not a goal from inspiration. Why do you want to make that amount of money? What would you do with that money? What would you love to do to make that money? Create a goal around those actions you'd love to do to earn the money or what you'll do with the money instead. This is how you can make it focused on what you love doing (inputs) rather than what you love doing it for (outputs).

You'll know you've created a goal from inspiration when it makes you feel expansive, aligned, fulfilled, and full of love. It will feel like you're feeding your soul instead of selling it.

A Guide to Feeling More Inspired in Your Work

Create a list of things you do in your work that drain you of energy—things that you don't like doing or that feel heavy overall. This is your energy-draining list.

Create a list of things you do in your work that give you energy—things that make you feel inspired, energetic, alive, and light. This is your energy-giving list.

Each week, eliminate one thing from your work that is on your energy-draining list and add one thing to your workday that is from your energy-giving list.

The goal is to get to a point where you're spending 80 percent of your work time doing things that are on your energy-giving list.

If you're not able to totally eliminate the draining task from your work, brainstorm ways that could make it more enjoyable for you. Sometimes the slightest shifts can make a world of difference in how we experience something.

Daily Journal

One of the best things you can do to help you on your journey to stop overthinking is to keep a daily journal to track your progress. Use it to note your thoughts, feelings, and behaviors without judgment. The more regularly you journal, the more helpful it will be to you. The insights you'll learn about your thought patterns, triggers, and modes of support will be invaluable on your path to non-thinking.

The following templates can be used as guides for journaling, but there is no need to follow a prompt or template if you find it unhelpful. Try writing freeform or using prompts that you create.

Use whatever works best for you and feels the most natural and achievable. Perhaps start with journaling for just five minutes a day. If you make this process too cumbersome, complicated, or long, it is less likely that you'll keep doing it.

living an abundant life
comes from following your fears
  instead of letting them control you

become curious about your fears
for they are the doorway to your dreams

Morning—Daily Intentions

Without a conscious intention to follow our intuition, we default to following our conditioning. This daily journal is designed to help you break free of this pattern by bringing your intuition into your awareness. It is best to complete this journal in the morning, as it will help set you up for a day free from overthinking.

*   *   *

What is my intuition telling me today?

When I ignore external influences and advice from anyone else, what does my intuition tell me to move toward? What is my intuition telling me to try? What feels most expansive, unknown, and aligned right now?

When I encounter fear and uncertainty today, how will I handle it?

Write a mantra to help you remember to trust and follow your intuition today.

Evening — Daily Reflections

These reflection questions are designed to help you become aware of the relationship between your thought processes (inputs) and the level of peace, love, and joy in your life (outputs). Positive emotions are our natural state when we let go of our thinking. Notice what happens when you focus your attention on the inputs instead of the outputs and how the outputs take care of themselves when you do so. It is best to use this journal in the evening, as it will help you reflect on your day and learn from your experiences.

* * *

Input/Cause Questions

Answer each of the following questions on a scale of 1 to 10, with 1 being the lowest and 10 being the highest. Then journal about your answer to provide more of a description.

How much was I able to let go of my thinking today?

How much did I follow my intuition today?

How much did I express my full, authentic self today?

How well did I manage my energy today?

How much did I follow what felt expansive, unknown, and aligned today?

How much of my attention did I focus on what I value most?

Output/Effect Questions

Answer each of the following questions on a scale of 1 to 10, with 1 being the lowest and 10 being the highest. Then journal about your answer to provide more of a description.

What was my level of peace today?

What was my level of joy today?

What was my level of alignment today?

How often was I in the present moment today?

How much was I in a flow state today?

Reflect

Now look at your inputs and outputs. Do you see a relationship between them? What impact did your inputs have on your outputs? What comes up for you after answering these questions? Do you see any patterns? What are your takeaways? What is your intuition telling you?

Resources

For easy reference, here are the helpful frameworks, charts, and examples from the book. Draw on these tools to help you on your journey to non-thinking.

How to Let Go of Negative Thinking: PAUSE

To help you remember the five-step process for letting go of your thinking, use the acronym PAUSE. Whenever you're feeling overwhelmed by your thinking, *pause* and remember that you have the power to let go of it at any time.

P—Pause and take deep breaths to calm your nervous system and ground yourself in the present. Become aware that you are thinking, but do not judge it.

A—Ask yourself, "Is this thinking making me feel the way I want?" or "Do I want to keep suffering?" If not, you always have the choice to let your thinking go in order to find peace.

U—Understand that you have the choice to stop and let go of it.

S—Say and repeat the mantra "Thinking is the root cause of suffering" to help quiet the mind from thinking until it subsides and passes.

E—Experience your emotions fully without judgment, resistance, or thinking (don't think; just feel).

Repeat this process until you have calmed your nervous system and the thinking has passed.

Thoughts versus Thinking: Examples

To illustrate the difference between thoughts and thinking, take a look at the following scenarios. In each, notice the difference between the initial reaction—the thought—and the negative rumination that occurs when one begins thinking about the thought. Thoughts are inevitable, but thinking about them is unnecessary.

Situation:

An event

Thought	Thinking
Neutral observation or intuitive prompting	Negative judgment or story about the thought

Situation:

It is raining.

Thought	Thinking
It is raining.	Why does this always happen to me?
	This is the worst.
	This ruined my day.

Situation:
You lost your job.

Thought	Thinking
I lost my job.	I'm not good enough.
	Everyone is judging me.
	I'll never recover from this.
	This is unfair.

Situation:
You arrive at work and find it unfulfilling.

Thought	Thinking
I want to quit my job.	What if I can't find another job?
	I might hate the next job even more.
	I'm not good enough to get another job.
	Why would anyone hire me?

Situation:
It is the weekend and you are deciding what to do.

Thought	Thinking
I want to start a new creative hobby.	It's a waste of time.
	I'm not creative.
	I'm not good at it.
	Other people are going to judge me.

Thoughts versus Thinking

The following chart compares different attributes of thoughts and thinking to help you identify which one is which within your mind.

Attribute	Thought	Thinking
Source	Universe	Ego
Charge	Neutral	Negative
Weight	Light	Heavy
Energy	Expansive	Restrictive
Nature	Infinite	Limited
Quality	Creative	Destructive
Essence	Divine	Mortal
Feeling	Alive	Stressful
Emotion	Love	Fear
Sense	Wholeness	Separateness
Effort	Effortless	Laborious
Root	Truth	Illusion
Time	Present	Past/Future

The Human Experience Equation

Our experience of reality is created from the combination of the events we encounter and what we think about them. To reiterate, our emotions come not from external events but from our own thinking about them.

Here is a more visual way to understand how our thinking can change our experience of an event through a simple equation:

Event + Same thinking = Same experience

Event + New thinking = New experience

What this equation means is that when we go through an event and think about it the same way we always have, it will always produce the same experience and therefore the same emotion. But if we change our thinking about that same event, we can alter our experience of it and create a new emotional response.

When you change your thinking, you change your experience of life—*without* needing to change the event that happened.

However, while we can change our thinking, the most ideal path to serenity is to let go of our thinking entirely. Without our own thinking about an event, we find peace because we are experiencing exactly what reality is without our own judgments, stories, or expectations of it. If we simplify the equation, we can see exactly this:

Event + Thinking = Perception of reality (suffering)

Event without thinking = Reality (peace)

Acknowledgments

Thank you, Sydney Banks, for sharing the principles you have discovered with the world. Because of you, I have found the truth within myself and now have the same privilege of sharing it with the world.

Thank you to my teachers and mentors, Joe Bailey and Michael Neill, for sharing your wisdom with me, which has changed my life forever. I am eternally grateful for your generosity and heart of service that keeps giving. Thank you for all you do and will continue to do for others.

Thank you to all my dear friends and family (Mom, Dad, Anthony, James, Christian, Bryan, and many more) for helping me discover my divinity and encouraging me to write this book. Without any of you, this book would not be in existence. Please know that because of you, the impact you have on me and anyone who will ever come across this book is immeasurable and will continue to change the lives of people all over the world.

Thank you, Kenna, for being one of the most loving and compassionate souls I have ever met and for showing me what true unconditional love is. I am in constant awe of your beautiful presence, and I can never thank you enough for the gift of your never-ending love for me and everyone you meet.

About the Author

JOSEPH NGUYEN is the author of the global best-seller *Don't Believe Everything You Think*. His work has been translated into more than forty languages and has touched the hearts and minds of readers worldwide. Drawing inspiration from philosophy, spirituality, and psychology, Joseph distills timeless wisdom into simple, pragmatic, and accessible books. Through his writings, Joseph illuminates the path to self-realization, guiding readers toward a life filled with abundance and liberation from emotional and psychological suffering.